W9-BKL-423

CAREER WISDOM

for College Students

Insights You Won't Get in Class, on the Internet, or from Your Parents

PETER VOGT

*Foreword by Doug Hardy,
Career expert and former editor in chief, Monster.com*

Ferguson
An imprint of Infobase Publishing

Career Wisdom for College Students

Copyright © 2007 by Peter Vogt

Ferguson
An imprint of Infobase Publishing
132 West 31st Street
New York NY 10001

ISBN-10: 0-8160-6837-2
ISBN-13: 978-0-8160-6837-1

Library of Congress Cataloging-in-Publication Data

Vogt, Peter, 1967–
  Career wisdom for College Students: insights you won't get in class, on the Internet, or from your parents/Peter Vogt; foreword by Doug Hardy.
     p. cm.
  Includes index.
   ISBN 0-8160-6837-2 (hc: alk. paper) 1. Vocational guidance. I. Title.
HF5381.V58 2007
331.702—dc22   2006024789

Ferguson books are available at special discounts when purchased in bulk quantities for businesses, associations, institutions, or sales promotions. Please call our Special Sales Department in New York at (212) 967-8800 or (800) 322-8755.

You can find Ferguson on the World Wide Web at http://www.fergpubco.com

Text design by Mary Susan Ryan-Flynn
Cover design by Salvatore Luongo
Illustrations by Sholto Ainslie

Printed in the United States of America

MP MSRF 10 9 8 7 6 5 4 3 2 1

This book is printed on acid-free paper.

TABLE OF CONTENTS

Foreword

I wish Peter Vogt had been my career counselor in college.

Back then, we started looking for work just around graduation time, which was about a year late. If any of us had visited the career center at school, we were given a list of books to read and an offer to chat with the one beleaguered career coach on campus. My friends and I also believed we knew "truths" about the job search:

"Your first job will determine the rest of your career."

"Don't use your personal connections to find work—that's cheating."

"If you just get the résumé perfect, you'll get the job."

"If you love what you're doing, you won't worry about the money."

"If you don't know your life's calling at age 22, you probably won't ever find it."

"If you're not premed or prelaw, you're pre-bum."

In retrospect, it is amazing to me that we believed these myths, which even then were far from the reality of work. But perhaps we can be forgiven because 1) the unemployment rate then hovered around a brutal 14 percent, and 2) career advice from parents and teachers generally reinforced the myths.

I, for one, spent a hot summer in a folding chair on the roof of a tenement building in Manhattan, reading *What Color Is Your Parachute?*, searching newspaper job ads, and blindly sending résumés off to possible employers.

In those days, career counselors were just beginning to suggest that instead of accepting a dreary, one-way vision of work,
students should broadly study jobs, industries, styles of working,
and the financial implications of their choices. Counselors also
caught on to the notion that students who knew more about their
own talents, interests, personalities, values, and temperaments
might more easily move toward careers in which they would be
happy and successful. They suggested this wildly original idea:
students entering the workforce should continue to be *students* of
the two most important factors defining success, the job market
and themselves.

What a notion! Students could continue to use the skills they
had earned with 16 to 20 years of effort (and pots of money) to
help decide the next phase of their lives! They could research the
job market, discover what they were good at doing, discover what
they *liked* to do, and thus make appropriate career decisions.
Just like researching a topic, testing hypotheses, doing fieldwork,
studying history, etc., in order to come up with a well-reasoned
conclusion in a term paper.

OK, that notion seems obvious enough today. But even now,
the experiences of countless students tell me it is hard to act on
these simple ideas. The fact is we do not yet educate ourselves
enough at the college level about careers. There are no semester-long courses on networking, or job research, or interviewing
skills. Professors can tell you a lot about their fields of study, but
blessed few can tell you how to prepare for the day-to-day work of
sales management, or health care administration, or technology
management. How many professors can describe the best career
progression for an airline pilot, a nursing supervisor, or a Web
interface designer?

This is not just a rap on colleges. Career centers have become
very good indeed. More teachers come to the classroom today
with real-world experience. In fact, students themselves are a big

part of the problem. When was the last time you saw a college career center crowded with students asking questions and making full use of the resources? When was the last time students circulated a petition demanding their college spend more money on career training, or that academic guidelines require every student to take two semesters of career management?

Now, fortunately, we have Peter Vogt, with his feet planted both in college career counseling and the real world. I have relied on his advice to college students for the past seven years, as he wrote his regular articles for Monster.com and MonsterTRAK. I have called on Peter to supply trenchant quotes for the *Monster Careers* series of books (written with Monster's founder Jeff Taylor). Peter knows your world, in which students start the job search from square one, and he knows mine, the new world of work in private industry, government, and not-for-profit organizations.

With *Career Wisdom for College Students*, Peter has finally brought all his insight and know-how into a progressive, A-to-Z guide for students just starting to make sense of the job hunt. Reading it, I am reminded that he is especially skilled at paring down the broad topics (like career testing or exploring different professions) to focus on the areas where students are most likely to stumble. You, as a person just starting out, do not have to become an expert in all matters of job search. You do not, for example, have to spend much time learning about midcareer changes! Yet most guides try to cover the whole range of possibility. Peter has focused on your situation alone.

As you will see, Peter grounds his advice in the experience of students he has known in a decade of counseling. This is also relevant, because they have entered the job market in a time unlike any in the past century. Work is becoming both more specialized and more interdependent. Globalization and the Internet have radically changed not only how business is done, but also how careers are built. At the same time, there are ancient truths that have been drowned in a rising tide of claims and chatter. Trust, honesty, and reputation still matter. Common sense, reliability, and judgment are more valuable than ever. Insight, self-knowledge, and critical questioning of one's beliefs are not only important to finding the right career, but they are hugely important in today's workplace, where the never-ending flood of information all too often substitutes for wisdom. Peter Vogt understands this, and the advice he gives in *Career Wisdom for College Students* is enlivened by the true stories of students he has guided through the exciting and scary early steps of learning to find work.

You need to be honest with yourself to take full advantage of this book. If you are not willing to do the homework that makes a real career possible, or if you do not want to discard your false assumptions, or if you would rather trust your luck, I suggest you try methods that don't work for a while, then return to Peter's book. As I learned on that hot rooftop decades ago, failure is a great motivator—to do things the right way.

If you have read this far, however, I will bet you have the energy to put into a real job search. It is one of life's true adventures, and Peter Vogt is a great guide along the way.

Hey, Peter, if you ever find a time machine, would you mind traveling back in time to work as a career counselor at my college, say, about 20 years ago? And if you don't have the time for a visit, will you at least send a copy of your book back to that rooftop in Manhattan?

—Doug Hardy,
Career expert and former editor in chief, Monster.com

Acknowledgments

A book *idea* doesn't become a finished *book* without the help of a whole lot of people besides the author!

I would like to thank, first and foremost, my wife Lois—not only for her constant emotional support during months of writing, but also for her nitty-gritty contributions to these pages. Whether I needed a fitting quotation, a Web address, or a statistic, you were there for me, Lois. I can't tell you how much I love you and how much I appreciate all the help you have given me on this huge project. All of this material is a rerun to you, I know, but you patiently watched the program anyway.

I would also like to thank my son, Isaac, who gave me permission to take a break from *Sponge Bob, Square Pants* once in a while so I could do some writing—alone. You are a good boy, Isaac.

Thanks to my parents, Charles and Nancy Vogt, and my siblings—Kathy Frost, Mike Vogt, and Mark Vogt—who all have supported me in whatever I do and have often ridden to my rescue to boot. Thanks as well to my parents-in-law, Marilyn and the late Merv Gessele, who have firsthand knowledge of the path of self-employment and thus understand its ups as well as its downs.

Many movie credits list the characters in order of their appearance in the film. My mind works that way when it comes to thanking people for their contributions to a book like this one. So from here on out, I will start from the very beginning and work my way to the present. Here goes …

To my high school English instructor, Mark Hassenstab—I am sorry for hassling you so much (it was the other boys' fault), but I appreciate your hanging in there with me and teaching me something about how to write. I still don't know why you never killed me or my partners in crime. Thanks for your restraint.

To my Moorhead State University instructors Melva Moline and the late Joe Dill—thanks for teaching me to think before I write. And to Shelton Gunaratne—you drove me and my fellow students nuts with your nitpickiness, but upon reflection I can only thank you for refusing to lower your high standards. I now know that the power of the written word was at stake.

To my old colleagues at *The Forum* in Fargo, North Dakota— especially Mark Hvidsten (the guy who taught me the day-to-day ropes) and Dennis Doeden (the guy who hired me). I may not have become a sportswriter, but that doesn't mean I didn't learn a lot from you all.

To my colleagues at Magna Publications in Madison, Wisconsin—Mary Lou Santovec, Charles Bryan, Doris Green, Robert Magnan, Linda Babler, and Marilyn Annucci. I appreciate your taking a chance on a fresh-grad rookie. And to you especially, Bob—thanks for teaching me how to actually think, whether it was over my keyboard or sitting across from you at the pizza place.

To my graduate school professors at the University of Wisconsin-Whitewater—especially Anene Okocha. Anene, I appreciate all you taught me, not only about career development but also about research. Brenda O'Beirne, you modeled what it was like to be passionate about one's career—something I had honestly never seen before—and Steven Friedman, you made the idea of conducting research somehow appealing. Thanks to all three of you for the expertise you lent during the challenging journey that is called the master's thesis.

To my colleagues and mentors at the University of Wisconsin-Whitewater Office of Career Services—Gail Fox, Carolyn Gorby, Jerry McDonald, and Kathy Craney, as well as Marge O'Leary, Eunice Lehner, Margaret Pelischek, and Kris Fantetti. How can I thank you all enough for what you taught me about the field of career services? Gail, a very special thank-you to you—for not only inviting me into the field of career development but also for encouraging me to stick around for a while. There is a book out there called *The Five People You Meet in Heaven*, which suggests that when you get to heaven you will be met by the five people in your life who had the most impact on you. I am certain, Gail, that you will be one of the five where my life is concerned.

To my colleagues and mentors at Edgewood College Career & Counseling Services—George Heideman, Shawn Johnson Williams, Janet Billerbeck, Merle Bailey, Sharon Boeder, Rose White, and Julie Bonk. I could not have been more welcomed or more blessed. George and Shawn, special thanks to both of you for not only teaching me about career issues, but helping me understand that I had knowledge and skills to contribute too. Thanks as well to several other Edgewood colleagues and friends who taught me so much—Jan Zimmerman, Maggie Balistreri-Clarke, Maureen McDonnell, Todd Benson, and Debora Barrera-Pontillo.

I would never have come up with so much to write about had it not been for my connection with the good folks at Monster and MonsterTRAK! Thanks in particular to Doug Hardy (Monster's former editor in chief), for writing the compelling foreword for this book. Thanks, too, to the fabulous content producers I have worked with over the years—Denis Gaynor, David Long, Kristy Meghreblian, Christina Lopez, Christine Stavrou, Ryck Lent, Christine DellaMonaca, Ann Pariani, and Norma Mushkat Gaffin.

I would also like to thank my current business partners with College to Career, Inc.—Terese Corey Blanck and Judy Anderson, as well as my partner in Campus Career Counselor, LLP, Pamela Braun. Bless you all for the gift of time—as in time away from other things to write this book. As important, thanks for your friendship and your insights, both for the book and for our continuing work together.

Special thanks to Barbara Winter as well. Barbara, I will never forget the key piece of wisdom you shared with me over coffee a while back: "Writing, Peter, involves putting words on paper!"

Thanks, too, to the many people who lent their insights, stories, or other assistance to *Career Wisdom for College Students*— Al Pollard, Megan Meuli, Rick Nelles, Carmen Croonquist, Lynne Schuman, Martha Krohn, John Krumboltz, Kathleen Mitchell, Russell Blanck, Michael Casarella, Elaine Thomas, Maggy Ralbovsky, and Exuper Okouya.

Thanks to my many career counseling clients, past, present, and future, for both your willingness to share your stories and your courage to tackle difficult career-related concerns. I admire you.

My thanks and gratitude as well to Jim Chambers and all his colleagues at Facts On File—editorial, design, marketing, and management—who have believed in this book from the start and brought it to life.

And last but not least, to all the good folks at the Caribou Coffee shop on the corner of France Avenue and Old Shakopee Road in Bloomington, Minnesota: Over the course of several months, you plied me with enough coffee to power a small city for a week. Fortunately I was able to channel that energy through my fingers and onto the keys of my laptop. Thanks for the free refills, the free electricity, and the free words of encouragement. I couldn't have done this without you!

Introduction

Knowledge is a process of piling up facts; wisdom lies in their simplification.

Martin Fischer

When I started overseeing the Career Planning for College Students message board on MonsterTRAK (http://www.monstertrak.com) back in 1999, I thought I would spend most of my time responding to relatively routine how-to questions: how to write a good résumé, how to do well in interviews, perhaps how to pick the right major or land a great internship, and the like. I also thought I would get most of my questions from college seniors and, especially, recent graduates. Posts from freshmen and sophomores, I figured, would be few and far between.

I was wrong—on both counts.

Sure, today's college students are asking their fair share of "how" questions where their future careers are concerned. I did the exact same thing when I was in college, especially right before and in the year or so after I graduated from Minnesota State University Moorhead in 1990. But lately—especially after the tragedies of September 11, 2001, the recession that followed, and the war in Iraq—I have sensed a significant change in the tone, substance, and timing of college students' career questions. The routine "how" questions have taken a backseat to the more troubling—and far more complex—"why" questions. Moreover, the "I've got time" attitude has taken a backseat to "I gotta get going … now." The college students of today aren't waiting until senior year or beyond to focus on their careers like … well, like I did when I was in college! They are starting as freshmen, or even as high-schoolers, either on their own or, increasingly, with a shove from their parents.

So as I was thinking about the career book I wanted to write for college students—the one you now hold in your hands—two things were crystal clear to me:

- My book would need to meet you where you are at right now—while you are still *in* college.
- My book would need to cover not only the "how to" but also the "why do"—as in:
  - Why do I need to bother learning about my interests, skills and abilities, values, and personality?
  - Why do I have to be careful about how I view my career decisions over the short and long terms?
  - Why do I have to leave college with experience under my belt? (And why do employers expect that anyway? We're talking *entry-level* jobs here—hello?)
  - Why do I need to work so hard to convince prospective employers of my skills and my self-motivation?
  - Why do I have to learn how to "network" when I can easily find job openings online or in the newspaper?
  - Why do I need to join a professional association in my field (especially when I am already basically broke)?
  - Why do the careers of today unfold the way they do, and why do the employers of today think the way they do?

Career Wisdom for College Students is my best attempt at covering the why along with the how—in a way you can use right now.

I begin in Part I by encouraging you to **Take a Look Around—a Real Look Around!** Perhaps the thought of learning more about yourself and exploring what is *really* out there in the world of work has never even remotely occurred to you. Well, now it has (or it will once you jump into Part I). Your college years represent your very best chance in life to go shopping when it comes to your career. If you are willing to look around a bit, you may quite literally end up pursuing a career tomorrow that you haven't yet heard of today.

In Part II, **Be Careful of What You Think You Know!**, I challenge you to identify the beliefs, assumptions, and perceptions you have about yourself and various careers, and to see the amazing power that various information source can have over your career decisions. One snotty comment from your otherwise harmless roommate could easily convince you to abandon the art-history major you have chosen; I have seen it happen. The same goes for the advice you get from your parents, the media, and elsewhere. Advice is wonderful—*if* it is accurate and relevant!

Part III of the book, **Build Your Skills and Experience through Hands-on Activities**, will teach you about the many ways you can pick up essential career-related experience while you are in college. It will also help you identify the critical skills you gain from those activities—the skills employers will be looking for when you are approaching them about jobs after graduation.

We wrap up in Part IV, **Land the Job You Really Want**, by discussing how you can get into the heads of prospective employers—and why it is so critical for you to do so during your job search. If you understand where an employer is coming from and why, you will be able to approach him or her in a way that makes you stand out from your peers, who will be busy *asking for something from* the employer instead of *offering something to* the employer … like you are.

I use the term "wisdom" in the book's title for reasons that are purposeful as well as personal: purposeful in the sense that the information in the book targets the *most critical* career issues you need to understand as a college student—the big-picture lessons you won't learn elsewhere—and personal in the sense that I wish someone had pointed these lessons out to me when I was in college. It would have saved me a lot of heartache—and it would have rescued me from moving back home with my parents for a few months after graduation, a time when I was one lost and depressed puppy thanks to my career ignorance. As I look back now, my lack of knowledge was understandable. But that did not make it any less painful, and it certainly made me wish I had some help. If *Career Wisdom for College Students* does nothing more than help you avoid the misery I went through—and the confusion I see among students each day on MonsterTRAK's Career Planning for College Students message board—then I will have more than accomplished my mission in writing the book.

And it is a mission as far as I am concerned. In the world of work you will sometimes hear the phrase, "It's nothing personal; it's just business." For me—whether I am talking to college students through the pages of this book, in my articles, the message board online, or even face-to-face—it is not just business, it is personal. Why? Because it was personal for me when I was in college, it continued to be personal for me when I became a career counselor, and it remains personal for me to this day as I interact with college students who are typically asking for nothing more than some guidance and perhaps a bit of empathy as well. I hope you will find both within these pages—and that you will share the career wisdom you gain along the way with all the (other) college students in your life, both now and in the future.

◆ PART I ◆

TAKE A LOOK AROUND— A REAL LOOK AROUND!

Introduction

Discover What Is *Really* Out There

> The only way of discovering the limits of the possible is to venture a little way past them into the impossible.
>
> Arthur C. Clarke

It is amazing how much we miss in life—how unaware we are of the activities and opportunities that surround us each day.

I sat outside for 10 minutes on a recent early fall day and tried to consciously observe what was going on around me. Several geese flew by first. It was hardly a new occurrence, especially in late September—but for the first time I took note of which direction the birds were flying and how well they were maintaining their V formation.

As I continued my watch, I also began to realize just how many cars go by on the nearby road each minute, each hour, each day. Every few seconds another car passed, driven by someone heading for who knows where to do who knows what with who knows whom.

Meanwhile, the red, yellow, and brown leaves rained continuously from the trees in the yard, floating to the ground to add to the crunchy mix of acorns that had already dropped from their perches in the oak trees.

All of this and much more happens in my world every day, just as it does for you. But I miss 99 percent of it—mostly because it almost never occurs to me to purposely seek it out in my own neighborhood, let alone the rest of my world.

This same phenomenon occurs when we are making career choices. We tend to investigate only the career ideas we are already aware of and know something about—mostly because it does not occur to us to look into the *unknown* careers in *unknown* areas or fields. With the best of intentions, we set out to "explore" different careers. But we tend to be terrible explorers, because we almost never leave our current career "neighborhood" to do our exploring (nor do we even carefully consider all of the careers that *are* in our own neighborhood). That is a shame—no, it is a tragedy—because the rest of the world, mysterious as it may be, offers a wealth of opportunities, one or more of which might be a perfect fit with our unique interests, skills and abilities, values, personality, and goals.

The *Dictionary of Occupational Titles*, published for years by the U.S. Department of Labor (until the late 1990s, when a slimmer version of the directory went online), listed brief descriptions of more than 12,000 different jobs that then existed in the world of work. Thousands of other occupations have developed since then that never found their way into the *Dictionary*'s pages. How many of these different jobs can you name? I don't know about you, but I would be fortunate if I could come up with more than a hundred off the top of my head. And even if I could, I doubt I would be able to offer accurate descriptions of what many of those jobs entail.

I have come to know how much I do not know about the world of work, even after years of studying it in depth. And I will bet that if you are honest with yourself, you will reach the very same conclusion.

Frustrating? Perhaps. But it is also exciting—because it gives me hope and confidence that there are satisfying jobs and careers out there for all of us, if we are willing to do the hard work of looking for them and learning about them.

Think of America's most famous exploration duo, Lewis and Clark. There is simply no way they ever had a conversation that went like this:

Lewis: "Where should we go next?"

Clark: "I dunno. Let's look at the map."

Lewis: "Map? What map?"

Lewis and Clark, after all, weren't using a map—they were creating one as they made their way through the American West. They were exploring in the true and accurate sense of the word, allowing themselves to simply discover what was "out there" without knowing ahead of time what that would be. You need to do the same thing—especially now, during your college years, which will likely be your best opportunity to look for new career doors and walk through them to take a peek.

Are you confining your career exploration efforts to the realm of the *known*—perhaps only two or three broad career areas or academic majors or job titles? If so, open yourself up to the idea of exploring the unknown as well—to really exploring in the true sense of the word. If, for example, you take a career assessment like the Strong Interest Inventory—which, when you are done, offers suggestions about careers that might be a good fit for you—do not immediately laugh off the careers that sound unrealistic. As important, do not skim past the careers you have never heard of either; one of them could be the one you have been looking for—if you are willing to give it the time of day.

If you are looking into a particular career field, do not focus solely on the one or two industry jobs you already know about. Think broadly. Ask industry insiders (in person or via phone or even e-mail) to fill you in on all of the jobs within the industry. Have them teach you as well about the related companies and industries they rely upon to do their work. Perhaps your calling lies in one of these peripheral organizations or fields.

College is the time to open your eyes and your mind, both in and out of the classroom. So start looking for the bigger picture in the world of work. For all the careers you already know about, there are probably dozens or even hundreds of careers—related and unrelated—you know little or nothing about. One of them might be the satisfying vocation you have been looking for. But you will never find out unless and until you are willing to explore—really explore—knowing that while your destination might be a mystery (for a while, at least), the journey will give you the many unexpected clues and ideas you will need to plot a fulfilling career course.

May that journey begin right now.

Look Inside

First Know Thyself—Now, Not Later

Ninety percent of the world's woe comes from people not knowing them-
selves, their abilities, their frailties, and even their real virtues. Most of us
go almost all the way through life as complete strangers to ourselves.

Sydney J. Harris

How can you tell whether you would like a certain career if you don't know what you are interested in—or could be interested in? How can you determine if you will succeed in a particular job if you haven't pinpointed what you are good at? How can you possibly figure out whether you will be satisfied in a given industry without understanding what satisfies you personally?

Answers: You can't, you can't, and you can't. You can *try*, of course, and every year thousands of college students do just that. Perhaps you land a coveted internship at an ocean-side aquarium, only to find that you—or, more accurately, your stomach—can't take the seasickness that comes with narrating whale-watching tours. Maybe you sign up to become a computer science major but discover one or two or even three years down the road that you can't handle programming. Or perhaps you call your parents in mid-May with the exciting news that you have landed the consulting job you always wanted, only to call them again in mid-July in the desperate hope they will have the solution to your misery.

One of the first career counselors on the face of the planet was the Chinese philosopher Lao-tzu. OK, he wasn't really a career counselor, but he easily could have been—especially since he offered advice like this, which is as wise and relevant today as it was then: "Knowing others is wisdom; knowing yourself is enlightenment."

"Enlightenment" probably sounds like a cosmic concept, and in some ways it is. (A quick trip through *Buddhism for Dummies* will tell you that.) But I think Lao-tzu might well have been thinking in literal as well as spiritual terms when he chose that particular word. What is the layman's definition of enlightenment? Quite simply, it means understanding something better because you can see it more clearly. It is hard to find your way in the dark. But if the road is "enlightened"—if only by a few streetlamps that make the signs easier to read and the landmarks stand out a bit better—you can get where you are going more quickly, and with more certainty that you are not headed in the wrong direction.

In all my years of helping college students with their career-related concerns, I can think of only a handful who actually wanted to work on essential *self-assessment* activities like identifying their interests, their skills and abilities, their values, their personality, their learning styles, and their short- and long-term goals. It is understandable; when I was that age, I didn't bother with these activities either. In fact, I didn't even know about them—although if I had, I doubt I would have pursued them. Sure, a test like the Strong Interest Inventory might be, well, interesting. But why screw around with that when you just want to hurry up and find a summer internship? It might be nice to have a better understanding of your natural abilities, but who has the time when you are taking a full load of classes, working 30 hours a week to pay for school, volunteering to get some experience in your field, and trying to repair a strained relationship with your significant other?

Self-assessment will probably never be the frontrunner on your list of essential college activities, and perhaps that is only natural given the hectic nature of today's college experience. But if you never get to self-assessment during your college years, it will come and get you later in life—probably unexpectedly and perhaps against your will, but it will get you nonetheless. It might show up when you are 23, only a few months into a job that you already can't stand. It may show up when you are 30, when the only phrase you can come up with to explain your on-the-job misery is "something's missing." Or maybe it will show up when you are 40 and you are asking yourself, "Is this all there is?" It is during these times when you will wonder where you went wrong and what you can do to change your situation. The answer in both cases: self-assessment.

If you are like most college students today, you thrive on checklists. You probably took advantage of a handy checklist when you were applying for colleges, to make sure you did what you were supposed to when you were supposed to. Perhaps you keep track of your core or general courses and the courses for your major by using a one- or two-sided checklist provided by your academic advisor or department. Those checklists wouldn't be much good if they did not have items on them, right? Well, self-assessment—whether you do it sooner (yes!) or later (noooo!)—allows you to put together the detailed checklist you need to make informed decisions about the major(s) you select and the career you ultimately pursue after graduation.

Suppose you had a one- or two-sided checklist that specified:

● Your top five interests

● Your top five skills and abilities

● Your top five career-related values

● Your top five personality traits

● Your top five goals

Wouldn't your checklist make it easy—or at least easier—for you to give the thumbs-up or thumbs-down to any academic major or career path you are considering? Perhaps you are thinking of majoring in anthropology. Read up on the field to see what it is all about, then go to your checklist: Do your interests seem to align with the interests an anthropologist might have? How about your skills and abilities? Would a career in anthropology allow you to do work that aligns with what is important to you (i.e., your values)? Consult your checklist to find out.

Without a checklist, you are flying blind—and at your own peril—when it comes to choosing a career. And without self-assessment, you have no checklist.

Years ago, there was a television commercial produced by a company that made oil filters. The mechanic in the commercial stressed the importance of addressing engine problems right when they begin—and while they are still inexpensive to fix—instead of putting them off and causing further damage to the car. At the end of the commercial, the mechanic offered an ominous warning: "You can pay me now, or pay me later."

When will you invest in self-assessment? The longer you wait, the more you will pay in the end.

Highlight This: You can't possibly know what career is best for you if you do not first figure out what you want, what you are good at, what is important to you, and what makes you tick.

This Is a Test; This Is *Only* a Test

Never let an assessment tell you what to do. Its purpose is only to give you some clues about your skills and interests. You've got to decide whether the clues are useful.

Richard Bolles

If a stranger were to ask you 10 questions about your life, could he then write a 400-page biography encapsulating your entire existence?

If you go on a date with someone new this weekend, will you know that person well enough by the end of the evening to ask him or her to marry you?

If you were to spend 20 minutes after class asking your political science professor about his views on socialism, could you then predict how he feels about every political matter that might come before him?

Of course not, of course not, and of course not. It is impossible—not to mention unwise and unrealistic—to merely ask someone a few questions and then define that person based on his or her responses.

Or is it?

If you are at a point in your life when you are exploring careers, you might well be inclined to turn to a career test—such as the Strong Interest Inventory or the Campbell Interest and Skill Survey or another tool—in hopes that it will tell you what you should do with your life. There is only one problem with this idea, but it is a big one: Career tests do not *tell* you anything, and they certainly cannot and do not define you.

I can hear your skepticism already. "But I just took the _____ inventory, and the thing told me I should be a ____," you might say. No, it did not. For starters, it did not *tell* you anything at all; it *suggested* some things. Moreover, it did not suggest what you should be or do; it suggested what you might want to consider being or doing.

These are not mere semantics. Indeed, if you do not learn and then acknowledge the limits of career tests, you are setting yourself up for confusion and misery.

Let us be clear: career tests can be very helpful. The best ones are well researched, well developed, and used with great care by the career counselors and others who offer them to college students. But think about it: Even if an inventory asks you 200 questions or more, is it really reasonable (or wise) for you to believe that the test can tell you what you should pursue as a career?

Career tests can be incredibly appealing, literally and figuratively. From a literal standpoint, the results you will get from a career test will often feature important- and official-looking charts and numbers, often in full color, almost daring you to believe that they are ironclad and not to be questioned. Figuratively speaking, when you feel like you are lost from a career perspective and you want to start finding your way, could anything be more attractive than the notion of spending 45 minutes answering a few questions, then kicking back and seeing what you should be when you grow up?

But here is the problem: You have to be careful where career tests are concerned. They definitely have their place in your career exploration activities. But they also have their weaknesses:

Career Tests Cannot Possibly Cover Everything. No test can ask you all the right questions. Moreover, no test covers each of the tens of thousands of jobs that exist in the world of work. It is simply impossible for test developers to highlight, for example, the job of *trout farmer. Accountant* is far less obscure and much easier to describe.

Career Tests Assume You Answer Each Question Accurately and Truthfully. Suppose you are taking an interest inventory that asks whether you would like to work with children at a summer camp, and that the responses you have to choose from are "Like," "Dislike," and "No preference/Don't know." If you are like many college students, you have never worked with children at a summer camp before, and so you may not really know whether you would enjoy it or not. Technically, then, you ought to choose the "No preference/Don't know" response. Guess what—you may be prone to offhandedly answer "Dislike" instead. Suddenly, your test results are skewed.

Suppose, similarly, that two of your siblings have worked with children at summer camps, and that your parents are pushing you to do the same even though you do not want to. You might be prone to choose the "Like" response to the question, even if you are unsure at best. On interest inventories in particular, it is easy to fall into the trap of responding to questions not in a way that is truthful, but instead in a way you want to feel or that you think you have to feel. As soon as that happens once or twice, your test results are skewed even more.

Career Tests Are Easily Misused and Misinterpreted. When I was in graduate school studying for my master's degree in counseling, I took a career development course in which we discussed the use of inventories in the career counseling process. My professor's warnings have stuck with me to this day: "Beware of 'test them and tell them!'" In other words, she was saying we career counselors have to avoid portraying career inventories as tools that can "tell" clients what to be when they grow up. Sadly, though, some counselors do just that, much to the detriment of their clients.

On the other hand, many more career counselors go out of their way to tell their clients about the limitations of career tests. Too often, though, the warnings go overlooked or ignored. You might hear your counselor say, "Remember, this is only a test." But you will still be tempted to take your test results home and complain to your roommate, "The dumb thing told me to be a banker."

Every once in a while—usually during your favorite TV show—the screen will go blank and a man with a deep voice will come on and say, "This is a test of the Emergency Broadcast System. This is only a test." If and when you sign up to take a career inventory—and especially when you get the results—keep this otherwise annoying man's voice in mind. It is yet another way that he might well save you in the event of an emergency.

Highlight This: Career tests do not tell; they suggest. They describe not what you should do but what you could do.

What Are You Good At?
Ask Someone Else!

> *You have skills and abilities that others do not. We often*
> *undervalue the things we know and what we can do, thinking,*
> *"If I can do it, anyone can." Well, "anyone" can't.*

Cathy Stucker

It makes almost no sense intuitively speaking, but it is true: Most of us are insanely bad at spotting—much less acknowledging—our own natural abilities and skills. I am starting to understand why. The things we do best are invariably things that come so easy to us that they cannot possibly—in our minds, at least—be of much use or value to anyone else, such as an employer, for instance.

I have seen example after example after example of this tragic phenomenon. When I was in graduate school studying for my master's degree in counseling, I led career planning sessions for groups of five to ten freshmen who were not yet sure what major or career they wanted to pursue. The most eye-opening activity we did in these sessions was called the *quality awareness* exercise. Each student in the group was given three identical copies of a one-page list featuring dozens of descriptors (personal "qualities") like these:

- Adaptable
- Competitive
- Decisive
- Imaginative

- Methodical

- Persuasive

- Resourceful

- Versatile

Each student had to take a copy of the list and circle all the traits she felt she had. She then had to give the other two copies to a couple of people who knew her well and ask them to circle the traits they felt she had. I did the exercise too; I filled out one of the worksheets myself, then gave another to my wife and the third to my supervisor at work and asked them to circle the traits they saw in me.

To be honest, the very first time I did this exercise I thought it was silly. It had a grade school "let's do a worksheet before recess" feel to it. But my mind was forever changed when we went over the results as a group, for those results came in two forms:

- **"They Do Not Realize I Am ... "** Once we had all filled out our own worksheets and gotten the completed worksheets back from our two compatriots, we were able to easily compile two columns of results. This first one featured all of the traits or phrases we had circled that our evaluators had not. I learned, for example, that I saw myself as "serious" even if my wife and supervisor at work did not necessarily see me that way.

- **"I Do Not Realize I Am ... "** The results in the first column were interesting, but the results in this second column were nothing short of profound. These were the traits or phrases that my two evaluators had circled that I had not. Example: I remember chuckling at, and then skipping right past, the word "articulate" as I was filling out my own worksheet. Yet both my wife and my supervisor had circled it. Suddenly, "articulate" was not funny anymore. "Maybe I *am* articulate," I thought to myself, "at least in some ways."

Invariably as we went around the room discussing the results in our career-planning groups, all of the students were able to share one or two traits they had not seen in themselves. Only when someone else had pointed out those traits did the students see them—and start acknowledging them.

The same thing has happened to me dozens of times in the years since, especially in my individual career counseling work with college students and recent graduates. The acting major I worked with—the one who thought she literally had no skills that would be valuable in a real-world work setting—began to understand that handling enormous pressure was a piece of cake for her, since she had acted and sung for large audiences at a major eastern university for four years, and had survived pressure-filled auditions along the way in order to earn the privilege. The journalism major I worked with began to see that her writing skills really were good enough to land her freelance assignments for a major local magazine (and, ultimately, a paying editorial assistant job at that same magazine). Even the fairly strong introvert I see in the mirror each day—me—has been told by several colleagues that he is good at building professional relationships through networking activities. Never would I have described myself that way.

We are all blind to our own best selves. And yet our best skills and traits often point forcefully, if not always obviously, to career possibilities that would be a great fit for us.

Do you know what your best traits are? Are you sure? Ask for opinions from a few of the people who know you best. What they point out might be hiding in plain sight, right in front of you— just waiting to be transformed into a rewarding career choice.

Highlight This: When it comes to your best skills and traits, you are probably oblivious to what is obvious to others.

Career Choice Goes Beyond What You Are Good At

It is the soul's duty to be loyal to its own desires.

Rebecca West

One of the first career counselors on the face of the planet—though I am sure he was not aware of it at the time—was Aristotle, the ancient scientist and philosopher who boiled career choice down to the following formula: "Where the needs of the world and your talents cross, there lies your vocation."

Much later, in the early 1900s, educator Frank Parsons— widely regarded in the career development field as the Father of Vocational Guidance—articulated a career-choice model that went like this:

> In the wise choice of a vocation, there are three broad factors: (1) a clear understanding of yourself, your aptitudes, abilities, interests, ambitions, resources, limitations, and their causes; (2) a knowledge of the requirements, conditions of success, advantages and disadvantages, compensation, opportunities, and prospects in different lines of work; (3) true reasoning on the relations of these two groups of facts. (Parsons, Frank. *Choosing a Vocation.* Boston: Houghton Mifflin, 1909.)

Formulas can be enormously helpful in life. Where would our society and our planet be, for example, without the chemistry formulas that drive medical breakthroughs or the physics formulas behind space exploration? Indeed, even in the far less complex world of career development, one of the easiest ways to match people up with jobs—as often happens in the military, for example—is to determine what their natural abilities are and channel them into jobs where those abilities are essential to success.

But just as formulas can literally change the world for the better, they can do significant damage if they are not exactly correct. And that is the problem with the formulas Aristotle and Parsons put forth: They are in the ballpark of being accurate, but they are not quite right. So if you follow them to the letter in hopes of finding the right career, you may or may not take the vocational path that is best for you.

Just how do the Aristotle and Parsons approaches fall short? After all, you are probably thinking, one's abilities do play a key role in the careers that person can and perhaps even should pursue. True enough. But here is the problem: Career choice goes beyond what you are good at. There are other factors at work, whether you know it or not, that will impact your career choice sooner or—much worse—later in your life. Among them:

Your Interests and Passions—What You Enjoy. Early in my college career, I learned through painful trial and error that what you are naturally good at (i.e., your abilities or *innate talents*) and what you enjoy doing are two very different things (see **Abilities and Skills ≠ Interests and Passions**, p. 22). What if, for example, your skills are well above average when it comes to writing, but you are just not all that fired up about writing as a life activity? To you, writing is something you can take or leave. It is a means to an end—something you have to do in order to accomplish something else, not something you want to do for its own sake.

A well-meaning adult in your life—one of your parents, perhaps, or a high school English teacher—might spot your writing ability early on and encourage you to pursue an academic major or even a career that involves a lot of writing. And you might easily and gratefully go along with the idea, figuring it makes perfect sense to choose a major and/or a career that seems to match up well with your natural talents. But sooner or later, your lack of passion for writing will catch up with you. If you are lucky, it will happen while you are still in college, giving you time to change majors and adopt a new direction for a future career. Sadly, though, you may not recognize this problem—or you might intentionally or unintentionally bury it—until years later, when you are already well into a career.

Can you change direction at that point? Sure. But you will be kicking yourself for not having made the abilities-interests connection sooner in life.

Your Values—What Matters to You. Maybe your natural gift for numbers and financial matters points to the possibility of a career in the high-powered and often lucrative world of investment banking. But as you step back and think about the day-to-day activities of an investment-banking job, you have trouble seeing how you would be helping people directly—especially people who may not have a lot of money themselves. Perhaps during your college years you participated in several Habitat for Humanity house-building activities, and maybe you enjoyed—more than you ever expected you would—being a resident assistant (RA) in one of the campus residence halls. These jobs paid you little or nothing in terms of money, but in your mind they made you rich in meaningful experiences. Just as important, they allowed you to contribute something valuable to the world and see firsthand the impact on real, living and breathing human beings.

Your abilities in this scenario are screaming at you to take one career path, but your values are cheering just as loudly for you to go in a vastly different direction. That fight is not going away.

Your Personality—What Makes You Tick. Perhaps you are a fairly gregarious and outgoing person who thrives on making decisions and taking action. Anyone who knows you well would describe you as a team-oriented "doer." You are a natural leader who is good at quickly gathering the opinions of others, making a choice, and running with it. No one would label you "indecisive" or "slow."

How will you thrive, then, working mostly alone in a research lab, studying a medical issue that hundreds of others have been studying for decades, and not knowing whether you will ever find The Answer in your lifetime? In that situation, how will you be the doer you have always been? And how will you make quick decisions and take decisive action like you have always done in the past? If you do not understand and acknowledge your personality—the traits that make you tick—you will be prone to pursuing careers that make you miserable most of the time. It would be a lot like writing left-handed if you are a natural righty: You could do it, but it would not be long before you were crabby about it.

So as you begin the often-complicated journey of exploring majors and careers, give thanks to people like Aristotle and Parsons who got the ball rolling when it comes to how best to make career decisions. But remember, too, that in many ways they were ahead of their time—and they were certainly ahead of your time. For there is much more to career choice than what you can do; there is also what you want to do, and why, and how.

Highlight This: What you are good at is just one piece of the career exploration and decision-making puzzle. You cannot—and will not—get a complete picture without the other pieces: your interests and passions, your values, and your personality.

Abilities and Skills ≠ Interests and Passions

I'd rather be a failure at something I enjoy than a success at something I hate.

George Burns

It took me nearly three years of college to learn the first meaningful career lesson of my life—even though I did not understand it at the time.

When I arrived on the campus of Moorhead State University as a freshman in the fall of 1985, I had already chosen a major: mathematics. Why? Because it was something I had been good at throughout my elementary and secondary school years, and everyone around me—parents, teachers, friends—kept pointing that out to me. So it only seemed logical, and reasonable, to select it as a major that would eventually lead to some sort of career.

Here is a quick look at how things went down(hill) from there:

First quarter of freshman year: Calculus I. No problem—practically a review of high school calculus.

Winter quarter: Calculus II. No problem—but not seeming to be terribly useful.

Spring quarter: Calculus III. No problem for the most part—but my questions and concerns about my major choice are multiplying.

Fall quarter of sophomore year: Calculus IV. Problem—this is getting hard. Then again, it is difficult to be motivated. Why do I need to do mathematical "proofs" when someone else has already proven this stuff years, decades, or even centuries ago?

Winter quarter: Math Foundations. Bigger problem—can this get any more boring?

Spring quarter: Vectors and Fields. Even bigger problem—it did get more boring, not to mention more difficult.

Fall quarter of junior year: Linear Algebra. Crisis unfolding—I do not get this stuff, nor do I want to.

Winter quarter: Intermediate Analysis. The end is near—I score a whopping 26 points out of 80 on my midterm (and even that was a gift). I withdraw from the course just in time to earn a grade of W instead of F—not yet knowing where I will go from here regarding my major.

What went wrong? I had been good at mathematics my entire academic life, and even during my worst times during college I had hung in there from a performance standpoint.

Problem: I hated mathematics. Bigger problem: You cannot hate something and expect to continue doing well in it. Worst problem of all: The aforementioned "problem" and "bigger problem" add up to career bewilderment.

In the spirit of my mathematics background, I offer you the essential point in the form of an equation:

Abilities and Skills ≠ Interests and Passions

In our American culture (and in many other cultures), we tend to point out to young people the things they are good at—or could be good at—and then suggest that they pursue those things as careers someday. "Boy, you are really good at _____," the well-meaning adults in our lives often say. "You should go into _____ someday." (See **Career Choice Goes Beyond What You Are Good At**, p. 18.) That is the advice I got in high school. And like thousands of other students—then and now—I followed that line of reasoning, figuring it made perfect sense. But some three years later, I (finally) discovered that something critical had been missing from what I had been told: If you are not at least interested in or passionate about what you are studying and eventually pursuing as a career, you are toast.

Do you see yourself falling into this same sinister (though understandable) trap? Then you need to make a change. You can fake your way through a major or a job for a while and probably even get away with it in the eyes of the outside observer. But sooner or later—sooner in most cases—your lack of genuine interest will catch up with you, leaving you confused, frustrated, angry at yourself, and perhaps even depressed. (Note: Depression is sometimes defined as "anger turned inward.")

Your abilities and skills play a key role in the major you choose and the career you will ultimately pursue. But so do your interests and passions. So the next time you hear, "Boy, you are really good at ____. You should go into ____ someday," translate that dangerous statement to, "Boy, you are really good at ____. Assuming you enjoy it, you should *consider* it as a potential major and/or career."

That is a longer equation, and it does not roll off the tongue quite as well. But it has a much better chance of adding up to fruitful, satisfying career exploration.

Highlight This: It is one thing to be good at something; it is a completely different thing to enjoy that something—especially enough to pursue it as a future career or course of study.

You Have to Live with *Your* Values

Change occurs when one becomes what she is, not when she tries to become what she is not.

Ruth P. Freedman

Practically all of us go through a time in our professional lives when we are torn between what we know we want and need in a career, and what others in our lives say we should want and should need. Sometimes these internal wars are the result of near-constant media exposure to a particular idea. If, for example, you watch TV for even half an hour, you will be pushed in all sorts of ways toward The Good Life as advertisers typically define it: a bigger car, a nicer house, a better body, the right beer. The bring-in-as-much-cash-as-possible-as-quickly-as-possible message is pretty relentless when you think about it—though too often, we do not even recognize it, let alone question it.

At other times, the career "shoulds" develop much closer to home—when a family friend harps on you to apply for a job at Company X, for example, or when your academic adviser says, "You will never get a decent job with a philosophy degree." The average college student's understandable reaction to these pressures is to cave in and go with the flow—to do what you are "supposed to do" and pick the "right" major or the "right" career. Why? Because it is the easiest, fastest way to stop the unwanted advice and criticism. But instead of solving all your problems, the path of least resistance generally makes them worse. The moment you deal with others' admonitions by going along with them, you inevitably start beating yourself up for selling your own wants and needs down the river: good-bye, outside "shoulds"; hello, self-inflicted "shoulds."

The only way to address the career "shoulds" once and for all is to identify *your* career-related values—whatever they may be—and then look for a career that does the best job of fulfilling *your* values. You will not be able to do that unless and until you first turn off the voices of:

Your Parents. Of all the people in your life, your parents probably have the greatest impact—for better or worse—on your career decisions. Perhaps your father has come right out and told you that the only way he and Mom will help you with your tuition is if you choose a "practical," "marketable" major like business administration or accounting. Maybe both of your parents have envisioned you as a doctor since the day you were born, while you have always pictured yourself becoming a writer or a musician.

The pressures can be strong enough in our generally individualistic, what's-best-for-me American culture. The weight of parental expectations can be nearly unbearable if you come from another culture that tends to value what is best for the group—and what is best for the group sounds revolting to you. For example, I will never forget the Japanese student I once worked with who could not bring himself to pursue his passion, graphic design, because his parents wanted him to go into finance. What is a student in that situation to do? What would you do?

These are fair questions, and there are no easy answers to them. But if you go into accounting for your parents' sake, who is going to be stuck doing your job every day? Your parents? Of course not; it will be you. Congratulations. You have won the battle, but you have lost the war big-time.

The parents of today's traditional-age (18 to 23 years old) college students are far more involved in the lives of their young-adult children than were the college parents of yesteryear. In a 2006 survey of 400 college students conducted by college job-search Web site Experience (http://www.experience.com), 25 percent of the respondents said their parents were overly involved, "to the point that their involvement is either annoying or embarrassing." Do your parents fall into that category, especially where your career decisions are concerned?

Your Friends. At some point, you just have to ask yourself a critical question: Is your best friend—the one who cannot even get to class on time or balance his own checkbook—your best source of career advice? Moreover, is your best friend so important to you that you will pursue the career he or she says makes sense for you?

Your Instructors. Your biology professor might mean well when she says you have a gift for understanding the intricacies of cell structure—and that you should thus consider becoming a cell biologist. To be sure, it can be flattering to get that kind of feedback from someone like a professor, who truly understands the skills necessary for success in a particular field. Unfortunately, though, your professor already has a job; she won't be willing or able to do your future job for you. Thus, the career path you ultimately choose had better be the one that fits you, not your professor.

The Media. The people you see on TV, hear on the radio, or read about in magazines will not be accompanying you Monday mornings while you ride the train to a job you cannot stand. You will be on your own. They may be telling you to chase all sorts of things via your career—money, power, status—and promising that happiness will soon follow. But just remember: You will be doing all the running in that rat race everyone is always talking about—and you will kick yourself hard when you finally figure out you have been running in the wrong direction for months … or even years.

Pinpointing what you value in a career is not easy; committing to pursue a career that allows you to live out those values is even harder. Unfortunately, you have no choice in the matter. You can ignore what is important to you in a career and get away with it for a while. Perhaps you are already well on your way to doing just that. Sooner or later, though—usually it is sooner—the disconnect between what you are doing for a living and what you value in a career catches up with you and starts hitting you hard. You have trouble motivating yourself to get out of bed and go to work in the morning. You tell everyone around you that "something is missing," though you cannot quite put your finger on what. You may even experience strange physical ailments—new aches and pains, a knot in your back that never goes away, insomnia, or extreme fatigue.

It is all the cost of doing business when it comes to trading away your own career values for someone else's.

Highlight This: Other people can tell you only what is important to them in a career; only you know what is important to you.

Don't Know What You Want? Then Start with the Opposite!

Reflecting on what you don't like can give you insights about what you do like.

Cynthia Petrites

I have worked with dozens of college students and recent grads who have come to me and said, in so many words, "I don't know what I want in a job or career." But I have yet to run into a single student or graduate who has had trouble telling me what he or she does *not* want in a job or career.

If you are feeling stuck—if you do not know what career possibilities you should explore given your abilities and skills, interests, values, and personality—one easy way to get yourself going is to identify the activities or characteristics you know you could not possibly stand in a job or career, and then work backwards from there.

Suppose I were to ask you the following question: "What do you want to *avoid* in your future career?" How would you respond? Perhaps you would make a list that looks something like this:

- I do not want to be stuck in an office all day, chained to the desk. That would drive me insane.

- I do not want to work alone—at least not very often. I do not want to feel isolated from other people.

- I do not want to do anything involving numbers. I suck at math.

- I do not want to do anything that involves a lot of writing. Writing is not my strongest suit.

- I do not want to work with people who are having troubles or issues. I just do not have the patience to deal with whiners.

(You will have your own anti–wish list, of course, but you get the idea.)

What You Want to Avoid in Your Future Career	It's Opposite—and Job/Career Possibilities to Consider as a Result
"I do not want to be stuck in an office all day, chained to the desk. That would drive me insane."	This suggests that you might enjoy a job or career that would give you lots of opportunities to work outside—literally. At a minimum, it points to a future job or career that allows you to be out and about—meeting with clients on-site, for example, or traveling by car or train or plane as a significant part of your work.
"I do not want to work alone—at least not very often. I do not want to feel isolated from other people."	This suggests that you will probably want to explore careers that are people-intensive where the work **environment** is concerned. You will want to look at professions for which teamwork is an essential skill—advertising, for example, or construction or entertainment.

"I do not want to work with people who are having troubles or issues. I just do not have the patience to deal with whiners."

This key point suggests that you will probably want to work with people who are not having troubles or issues! Thus, careers like counseling or customer service may not be worth exploring right now, whereas careers like sales or public relations might make more sense.

"I do not want to work with people who are having troubles or issues. I just do not have the patience to deal with whiners."

These conclusions—combined with "I do not want to work alone"—point again toward jobs or careers that focus mostly on people and relationships and less on gathering and crunching data or communicating in writing.

Now, take each point you have written on your list and try to identify its opposite. Sometimes this will be easy, other times it will be quite tricky. Just do the best you can for now. Here is how things might look using the list above:

This is not a perfect approach, and it certainly will not help you come to any immediate conclusions about the career you should ultimately pursue. But that is not the point. Right now, you are exploring careers. All you need is a strategy that will help you look around a little more purposefully in the beginning—a tool that will get you unstuck and on your way down a much more extensive and intensive path of career exploration. By examining what you know you will hate in a future career, you begin to pinpoint—albeit indirectly—what you will love in a future career. And that is one of the first key steps to finding a career that does fit.

Highlight This: You can figure out what you enjoy and what you want by identifying—and analyzing—what you do not enjoy and what you do not want.

Look Outside

Career Information Is Just a Page or Two Away

A bookstore is one of the only pieces of evidence we have that people are still thinking.

Jerry Seinfeld

Even though the World Wide Web is an outstanding, and in many ways astounding, resource for anyone who is exploring careers, it has its downsides:

It Is Not Always Well Organized and Thorough. Web sites are produced by experts, morons, and everyone in between. To say that quality control is lacking at times is an understatement. Even if you can find something you are looking for on a particular Web site, it is not at all certain the information is sound.

It Is of Practically No Use to Anyone Who Lacks Search Skills. Many people who use the Web—including a surprising number of college students—have limited or nonexistent skills when it comes to understanding how to search for information efficiently and effectively. Someone out there may have a Web site that could win the Pulitzer Prize, but if you cannot find it, that site is useless to you.

It Is Almost Always Great for Breadth, but It Is Too Often Lacking in Depth. With even the most rudimentary of search skills, you can find Web sites on almost any subject you can imagine. But in many cases, the sites you find cover only the basics of the topic at hand.

It Does Not Lend Itself to Saving and Easily Revisiting Information. Don't get me wrong: It is simple enough to "bookmark" information from the Web, and it is not even that difficult to organize your bookmarks into folders and subfolders on your computer. But even when you are finished with the bookmarking and organizing process, the only way to go back through the information you have saved is to revisit each of the sites or pages you have found along the way, one by one by one.

You Cannot Carry It Around. Sure, the Web is as close as your notebook computer, your handheld palm computer, or even your cell phone. But you still have to find wireless or wired Internet access, and if you do not want to haul around your notebook, for instance, suddenly the information you want right now is at home with your computer.

Ironically, It Makes Browsing Difficult. Internet Explorer, Netscape Navigator, Mozilla Firefox, and similar software programs are known as Web *browsers*. Oddly enough, though, you cannot really browse with them—not the way you would browse through CDs at a music store, for instance, or browse through blouses on a clothing rack or even browse through used cars at a used car dealership. Browsing, by definition, means quickly pawing through many items at once. No matter how skilled you are at finding information on the Web, ultimately you can see and read only one Web page at a time. Sure, you can click from page to page to page, but it is difficult to see the big picture at a glance.

You will be shocked to learn the antidote to these World Wide Web weaknesses: books. Yes, the book is alive and well, and for good reason. It still has an important role in the world of information gathering and distribution. Why? Because it sidesteps all of the problems above and then some, whether the topic is career exploration or something else. To wit:

Most Books *Are* Organized and Thorough. The companies that publish nonfiction books expect the authors they work with to do the best job they can of organizing their thoughts into a coherent package. Publishers also expect their books' authors to include—and cite—outside sources as appropriate. Once a publishing company has a book manuscript in hand, that manuscript goes through several editors. The overarching goal of the process is to develop a high-quality, highly reliable publication that readers can trust.

Most Books Require No Search Skills of Any Kind. Clearly, you need to be able to find the right book in the first place—which may involve a quick Web search or a one-minute chat with the reference librarian at your local library. But once you have a book in hand, the only search strategy you need is the ability to read through the table of contents and/or the index.

Most Books Offer *Both* Breadth and Depth. If a book lacks either depth or breadth, it might not be a book at all; it might be an *article*—at best.

It Is Easy to Save and Revisit Information in Books. Unless you lose things easily, it is pretty difficult not to save the information available in a book. Keep the book, keep the information. And if you want to revisit a piece of information you looked at before, just turn to the appropriate page or pages. If you highlight key passages or paragraphs along the way, it will be even easier for you to find key points again later—even if you do not return to the book for months or years.

You *Can* Carry Books Around. Enough said.

Browsing Is Easy. You can take two important angles where books and browsing are concerned. For starters, browsing through one particular book is as simple as flipping through its pages and seeing if anything catches your eye. But there is a bigger picture that is even more important where your career exploration is concerned: Go to any decent-sized bookstore or library and head for the Careers section. As you stand in front of the dozens or even hundreds of books before you, you can easily begin exploring career possibilities by reading the titles on the books' spines—to say nothing of the contents inside the books themselves.

So while you will continue developing your relationship with the World Wide Web today, and you will undoubtedly make the acquaintance of some new information-gathering technologies tomorrow, do not forget yesterday's dear old friend—the book. Like your lifelong pals in real life, books offer something unique to your career exploration that other tools simply cannot.

Highlight This: When it comes to career exploration tools, books outshine their competitors in too many ways for you to ignore.

Talk to People—That's 'People,' Not 'Person'

*A prudent person profits from personal experience, a wise one from
the experience of others.*

Dr. Joseph Collins

During my counseling practicum at Edgewood College in
Madison, Wisconsin, I once worked with a student who was
interested in becoming a nursing major. She knew a little
about the field—she had heard, for example, that there was a
nursing shortage at the time (which was true and still is)—but
like many students, she felt she needed some more information in order to make an informed decision about whether the
field was for her or not. Very smart.

So I encouraged her to do some reading about the field and,
especially, to talk to some local nursing professionals about
their work. Through these *informational interviews*, I advised
her, she could get the inside, from-the-trenches view of the
field that no book or Web site could ever provide.

"Good idea," she replied. And off she went.

A week or two later, she was back in my office. Nursing was
not for her, she had concluded—especially after her informational interviewing experience.

"Who did you talk to?" was my natural question. But the
more relevant question would have been, "How many people
did you talk to?"—for she had done informational interviews
with a grand total of one nurse, and she had chosen a jaded
veteran nurse at that. That nurse had painted a 100 percent,
utterly negative picture of the field of nursing, and my student

not only bought that picture but also decided not to shop elsewhere for other pictures. Not very smart.

I pointed out to the student that the idea behind informational interviews was to focus on the "s" in the word "interviews"—as in "talk to *people*," not "talk to *one person*." She nodded her head in apparent agreement. Intellectually, she was with me. But psychologically, her mind was already made up: nursing was not for her.

Now, perhaps this student would have ultimately decided against nursing anyway, no matter how many nurses she might have consulted. Maybe she was never truly interested in the field in the first place but was instead simply compelled by visions of an almost instant, well-paying job after graduation. But I—and more importantly she—will never know, because she did not bother to go beyond one viewpoint in her informational interviewing activities.

Informational interviewing is one of the best things you can do to explore a potential career. But just as a one-source research paper will likely earn you an F from your history professor, a one-source informational interviewing strategy will likely lead to failure to understand a particular career from all angles. And it will be a shame if you then eliminate that career from consideration.

Any person you meet for an informational interview is, well, a person—a human being with feelings, biases, and experiences both fresh and ancient. You have no idea whether your informational interviewee fought with his wife before your meeting, or just got screamed at by his boss, or has to fire someone right after your meeting with him is over. You also have no clue as to what he has seen in his years in the field, working for and with various people in various organizations. It all adds up to *his* view of the world and of the field or industry you want to learn more about. It is *his* reality, not *the* reality.

That is why it is so critical for you to talk to several people when you are exploring careers or industries. Talk to people who have been in the field for years; talk to those who just started a year or two ago. Talk to people who work in large organizations as well as small ones. Talk to men; talk to women. Talk to people in various specialty areas. Talk to people in for-profit companies as well as nonprofit entities. Talk to alumni of your school or your specific academic department, and talk to alumni of other institutions too.

There is absolutely nothing wrong with talking to someone who is less than happy with his or her job. After all, you want to hear the bad with the good when you are trying to decide wisely on a career path. But all bad or all good based on one person's viewpoint is inaccurate and potentially dangerous. It could lead you into a career that really is not for you or, perhaps more tragically, compel you to eliminate an option that could have turned into a rewarding career.

What is worse: investing a little more time and energy now to get a wide-ranging look at the career you are considering, or later regretting the time, energy, and perhaps money you have devoted to a career that turned out to be entirely wrong for you?

Highlight This: You are looking for trends when exploring careers—not one person's opinion, but a general consensus. There is no such thing as a consensus of one!

You Do Not Need to Talk to People in Person

National borders aren't even speed bumps on the information superhighway.

Tim May

If you want to talk to people to learn about careers (see **Talk to People—That's 'People,' Not 'Person'**, p. 37), you need not be limited by geography—not anymore, at least. All you need is an e-mail account, an inquisitive attitude, and a little creativity—like Exuper Okouya, a French citizen attending college in Canada, whom I learned about a few years back.

Exuper posted a message to the Career Planning for College Students discussion group I oversee on MonsterTRAK (http://www.monstertrak.com), the college student and recent graduate Web site of leading online career site Monster. In that note, Exuper briefly mentioned how he had conducted informational interviews with people from two countries without leaving his home near the University of Quebec.

It all started when he read an article in *Fast Company* magazine that described trends in management consulting. Several consultants had been interviewed for the article, and their e-mail addresses were listed at the end of the piece. Exuper was exploring consulting as a career possibility, so he got an idea: He would e-mail all of the people who had been featured in the article and ask if they would be willing to answer—via e-mail, naturally—a few questions about the field. He also began gathering the e-mail addresses of other management consultants by visiting various career and industry Web sites.

Over a period of about three months, he later told me in an interview (which I conducted by e-mail—surprise, surprise!), he ended up sending inquiries to 30 consultants in the United States and Canada. Fourteen of them responded to Exuper's request and said, in effect, "Sure, ask away!" And so ask Exuper did. He ended up obtaining not only useful insider information about the field but also, just as importantly, contact information for several consultants in his neck of the woods, Montreal. That gave him the chance to check out the management consulting market locally, too.

Nothing Exuper did was rocket science. He simply used his creativity and ingenuity to get the career information he wanted and needed. You can do the exact same thing. The only thing standing in your way is the accumulation of some names and e-mail addresses. And that's not a problem. You can track potential interviewees down through all sorts of channels:

Your School's Career Center. Many campus career centers around the country have extensive databases featuring current contact information for hundreds or even thousands of alumni, who have typically volunteered to serve as informational interviewees for current students (see **Your School's Alums Will Probably Help You—but Only If You Ask!** p. 54). Often, you can search these databases by topic and/or geographic area. Need to talk to an alumnus who is a financial planner in a state halfway across the country? Just select the right database criteria and you will have someone's name—and e-mail address.

Professional Organizations. Practically every career that exists has an association of some type made up of people who work in that field. Suppose you would like to talk to some people who work in training and development, for example. If you visit the Web site of the American Society for Training and Development (www.astd.org), you will be able to find the names and contact information of various leaders of the organization at the national level. If you want to, you can then search the site for links to state or local ASTD chapters—where you will find even more names and contact information. (You will soon discover, as a bonus, that people who are leaders in professional organizations tend to be more receptive than most when it comes to talking to college students about their fields. Why do you suppose they are leaders, after all? They take on their association roles, in part, to promote their professions.)

Magazines, Newspapers, and Other Publications. Like Exuper Okouya, you can develop a list of potential informational sources by reading articles in various publications, listing the people who are interviewed for those articles, and tracking down their contact information via, for example, a Google search http://(www.google.com) or with the help of a reference professional at your campus library. If you were a working professional, wouldn't you be apt to respond positively to a college student who e-mailed you and wrote something like this?

> I saw the article about your company in the *Atlanta Business Chronicle* the other day and immediately became curious to learn more about what you do in the field of logistics. Would it be OK for me to e-mail you a few questions about your work and how you got to where you are today?

Company/Organization Web Sites. Visit some company or organization Web sites and you will get the feeling that they are intentionally hiding employees' names and contact information! (Probably true in some cases.) But many organizations—especially smaller ones—do just the opposite: Names, contact information, even photos in some cases are freely available to anyone who visits the company's Web site. All you have to do is look.

And even if you cannot find the e-mail address of the person you would like to talk to, you can often take an educated guess at it. Just look for the e-mail address of someone else at the company—someone who works in media relations, for example. If his address is John.Smith@Company.com and you are looking for the e-mail address of Beth Miller, chances are her address is Beth. Miller@Company.com. Give it a try; the worst that will happen is that your e-mail will bounce.

Thanks to technology, you can conduct informational interviews with practically anyone who is willing, in any part of the world. All you have to do is let your fingers do the talking.

Highlight This: Thanks to technology, your informational interviewing activities need no longer be limited by geography. If you cannot talk to someone in person, see if you can talk to him or her via e-mail.

Lurk and Learn: Internet Listservs Open Your Eyes to New Possibilities

Let your hook always be cast. In the stream where you least expect it, there will be a fish.

Ovid

Wouldn't it be great if you could find out more about a career of interest by convening a meeting of dozens or even hundreds of professionals in that field—right in your own residence hall room or apartment?

Thanks to today's technology, you can do just that. You do not even need to have or use the newer tools at your disposal—instant messaging, podcasting, and the like. Indeed, you can turn to an old, reliable friend: your e-mail account. Just subscribe to the right Internet *listserv* and "talking" to diverse professionals in your field of interest will be as simple as typing a note and clicking the "send" button.

I am always surprised by the lack of knowledge college students have regarding listservs. If you are like many students I have worked with, you have either never heard of listservs or never bothered with them. You spend most of your technological time IMing, messing around in chat rooms or on social networking Web sites, or talking with friends and family on your cell phone. That is all fine. But if you are not tapping into listservs—particularly for career development purposes—you are missing out on one very easy way to position yourself nicely for your postgraduation future.

A listserv is the electronic equivalent of being in a room with a large group of people. The members of a listserv—known as the *subscribers*—have signed up for the ability to communicate with the other listserv members via e-mail. Specifically, each time someone on a listserv sends an e-mail message to that listserv, all of the subscribers receive it. Those subscribers can then read the message and, if they want to, reply to it with another message—which once again goes to all the listserv's members. Before long, you have an electronic "conversation" going, often with people from all kinds of backgrounds working in all kinds of locations across the country or even around the world.

Even if you never reply to a listserv message or post one yourself—you simply "lurk," as the strategy is typically called—you benefit in several tangible ways:

You Get a Sense for What Is Happening—and What Is Urgent—in a Particular Field. I am on a career counseling listserv called Professional Jobtalk. Practically every day, members from around the country post questions, share insights, and spread word about emerging trends in the field of college and university career services. All I have to do is read the messages and absorb the information. Over time I end up becoming more informed about what is going on and about what is of pressing importance in my field. You can reap similar benefits by joining a listserv in whatever field intrigues you.

You Become Familiar *with* People Who Are Considered Leaders in the Field. Spend a few weeks on any listserv and you will soon discover that several members tend to contribute the most to the ongoing discussions. You could contact one of these professionals directly at some point to get advice or ask specific questions of your own. Who would not be impressed if you were to introduce yourself like this?

> I saw your recent posting on the ___ listserv and I was intrigued by your extensive background in ___. Would it be OK if I were to e-mail you a few questions about ___?

You Become Familiar *to* People Who Are Considered Leaders in the Field. Once you get comfortable being a member of a particular listserv, you may decide to reply to a message or two, or even post a new one (or two or three or four) of your own. Congratulations! Now, people who are working in your field of interest will get to know you a bit. At a minimum they will see that you are fairly serious about the field. (If you weren't, they will conclude, then why would you bother being on the listserv in the first place?) Moreover, they will begin to "recognize" you after a while, to the point where they might believe they actually know you. (I cannot tell you how many times I have gone to a professional conference and run into someone who says, "Peter! I know you from the Jobtalk listserv!")

You Get First—and Often Only—Notice About Job or Internship Openings. To most employers who are looking to hire for an open position, an ad in the newspaper or on an Internet job site is the absolute last resort. They would much rather hire someone they personally know, or hire someone who comes highly recommended by someone they personally know and trust. That is why job (and internship/co-op) postings are frequent on practically any career-specific listserv you will find. You will not see them, though, unless you join a listserv yourself.

It is not difficult at all to find and join a listserv. Many professional associations have their own listservs. You will also find thousands of possibilities on sites like Yahoo! Groups (http://groups.yahoo.com), which typically have simple tools you can use to search for listservs by topic.

Once you have identified a listserv to join, it is typically as easy as following directions and sending a blank e-mail message to a specified listserv address. Within minutes (in most cases, at least), you will be on board—and ready to convene those career information meetings from the comfort of your beanbag chair.

Highlight This: By joining an Internet listserv that is related to your field of interest, you will learn more about the industry, get to know some of its key players, and—hopefully—help some of those key players get to know you as well.

Use Professional Associations to Explore Careers

Knowledge is of two kinds: We know a subject ourselves or we know where we can find information upon it.

Samuel Johnson

Pick a career, any career. With very few exceptions, the career you have chosen is connected with a *professional association* made up of dozens, hundreds, or even thousands of its practitioners—be they from a single city, a state or broader region of the United States, or an entire country. Whatever the occupation, people in that occupation tend to eventually find ways to come together so they can share resources and ideas with each other and the people they serve.

Some professional associations, like the American Medical Association (http://www.ama-assn.org), are huge and very well-established. Others, like the Association of Storage Networking Professionals (http://www.asnp.org), are comparatively small and perhaps just getting their wings. And, of course, most professional associations are somewhere in between. But no matter what their size, all professional associations share at least one common goal: to promote the career they represent and keep it growing—in terms of both numbers and scope.

One common way for professional associations to pursue that worthy goal is to create career exploration materials for people who are interested in learning about the field and how to get into it. If "people" here sounds like you, you are right! Often, a professional association's career materials are geared specifically toward you, the college student. All you have to do is be aware of the existence of these materials—and then go looking for them. Here are just a few examples of what you might find with only a modest investment of your time and energy:

Career Brochures. Many professional groups have developed simple three- or four-panel brochures that describe the basics of a particular career. These days, you can almost always access these brochures (in PDF format) for free on an association's Web site. At a minimum, you can call or e-mail the association and request a hard copy be mailed to you.

Web Pages or Sites. The typical professional association devotes at least part of its Web site to general career information, which you can easily read on-screen or print and read later. Some larger associations go a step further and develop separate Web sites—with separate URLs—that feature not only basic career information but also job openings for people who are already working in the field. The Society of Fire Protection Engineers (http://www.sfpe.org), for instance, produces the Fire Protection Engineering Web site at http://www.careersinfireprotectionengineering.com.

Online Profiles and Contact Information. Some professional groups feature online profiles of various members working in various jobs for various organizations. You might be able to read, for example, about one accountant who works for a large public firm, another who works for a small nonprofit, and a third who is self-employed. On occasion, the names and contact information of the people profiled (or others in the organization) are included on the association's Web site so that, if you would like, you can contact them (via phone or e-mail) to ask them questions about their work. (Note: Often, professional associations also list the names and contact information of their current leaders. Even if this information does not appear in the Careers section of the group's Web site, you can still contact these folks to see if they would be willing to share career advice with you.)

Shadowing and Internship or Co-op Information. Are you the type of student who explores careers (or anything else) best by *doing*? If so, you will be glad to know that many professional associations develop and promote experiential learning opportunities for college students. Some offer *shadowing* programs, which allow you to follow a working professional around in his or her job for a day (or two or three) to see what it is like. Other professional associations sponsor or publicize internship and co-op programs for students—in great part because the organizations know that today's successful intern or co-op student is often tomorrow's full-time, successful hire.

Books and Other Publications. If you visit the Web site of the American Psychological Association (http://www.apa.org), you will find information on its highly regarded book, *Career Paths in Psychology: Where Your Degree Can Take You*. On the American Sociological Association's Web site (http://www.asanet.org), you can download a free PDF of the informative study *"What Can I Do with a Bachelor's Degree in Sociology?": A National Survey of Seniors Majoring in Sociology*.

It is comparatively rare for you to find people (or groups) who not only say they want to help you with your career exploration, but who also demonstrate it by welcoming you with open arms. Sure, you will run into the occasional, er, grump when you contact a professional association. Far more often than not, though, you will instead connect with a person or people who, in some ways, are almost as invested in your future career as you are, because you may end up being their trusted colleague in the field one day, contributing your own time and expertise to ensuring its future.

Highlight This: Professional associations exist to promote their industries—especially to college students like you, who represent the futures of those industries. So look for and take advantage of the career exploration resources available through professional groups.

The Hidden Treasures in Career Center Placement Statistics

Things don't turn up in this world until somebody turns them up.

James A. Garfield

Of all the questions I receive as a career counselor who works primarily with college students and recent grads, one in particular stands out as being the most common by far. It goes something like this: "What can I do with a major in _____?"

In other words, what type of future job can you get with a psychology degree, or a biology degree, or a cultural anthropology degree, or a _____ degree? Often, the student or grad who asks this question envisions a detailed, comprehensive directory "out there" somewhere, identifying each and every job that might result from each and every college degree in existence. Unfortunately, The List—as one exasperated career services colleague once called it—does not exist. But something awfully close is available to you as a student. And it is often hiding in plain sight at your school's career center (or, these days, on its Web site).

It is usually called the career center's annual *placement report*, though it goes by various other names too (e.g., *annual report, graduate job summary*). In a nutshell, it describes the types of jobs landed by recent graduates of your school. Often, it also notes where (in terms of both city, state, and organization name) those grads landed jobs and, on occasion, what their starting salaries were and which job-search method (e.g., networking, on-campus interviewing, an Internet Web site) ultimately landed them their current position.

Where does all this fabulous information come from? The graduates themselves. Typically, the career center (or another department on campus, such as the alumni office or the institutional research office) surveys the new class of graduating seniors shortly before graduation day, on or near graduation day, and/or three to six months after graduation day. Some schools mail hardcopy surveys to the new graduates. Others use e-mail or a secure Web-based system. Whatever the method, the overriding goal is the same: to gather as much job-related data on as many new graduates as possible so that continuing students—like you—can learn from the students who have gone before them.

Would it help you to know, for example, that among last year's graduates of Anywhere University who responded to the career center's placement survey:

- Seventy-four percent of the English grads found jobs in their field within two months of graduation?

- The median starting salary for accounting grads was $37,600?

- The organization that hired the most grads from your school was Company X?

No matter how many books you might read or Web sites you might visit looking for detailed information on majors and careers, nothing beats the school- and often even major- or department-specific data you will find in your own school's placement report. Take, for example, the online brochure *What Happened to the Class of 2004,* a comprehensive survey of 2004 Monroe Community College (New York) graduates conducted by the school's Office of Institutional Research (see http://www. monroecc.edu/depts/research/grad/brochure2004.pdf). Want to get a sense of how students in radiologic technology fared? Twenty-seven students graduated from that program in 2004, 25 responded to the Institutional Research survey and of those, 18 were employed full-time. The median salary of the 13 grads who provided salary information: $34,000, with a low-end salary of

$30,000 and a high-end salary of $58,240. You are just not going to find career information that is more thorough—and personally useful—than that.

Unfortunately, career center and other college or university staff run into a number of aggravating problems where their graduate surveys and placement reports are concerned—problems that can have a direct impact on you. For starters, some campus career centers simply do not have the staff and other resources they need to do justice to the surveying process. Indeed, some campus career centers do not even bother trying to survey new grads, and many of those that do end up with data that are not terribly useful or reliable.

Another frequent problem focuses on marketing (or lack thereof). Sometimes campus career centers have outstanding placement data to share with current students, but they do not have the resources to raise student awareness of that information. These career centers make the data freely available on their Web sites, and some even print hard copies for distribution to students who walk into the career center. But too often students still have no idea the information exists.

On the other hand, you might be fortunate enough to attend a college or university that does have useful placement statistics and that has found effective ways to get that information into the hands (and minds) of students. If that is the case, you are lucky—to a point. You need to be careful, and a little bit skeptical at times, to see the information for what it is and what it is not. One key question to ask about any placement data you see: What was the response rate in the survey(s) that generated the information? Suppose you are thinking about a major in psychology, for example, and this past spring 100 psychology majors graduated from your institution. You are glancing through the annual placement report and you see that "80.0%" of the psychology majors landed jobs within three months of graduation. "Interesting," you might think to yourself. "Eighty out of 100 got jobs."

Not necessarily. For upon closer inspection, you see that only 60 of the 100 psychology graduates responded to the career center's placement survey. In other words, the "80.0%" figure is 80 percent of 60 (i.e., 48 graduates out of 60)—and not 80 percent of 100 (i.e., 80 graduates out of 100). That in itself is a big difference. But much more important is the follow-up question you must then ask yourself (and the career center):

> What about the other 40 psychology graduates—the ones who did not respond to the survey? What became of them? And why didn't they respond to the survey? Is it because they are so angry that they did not find jobs?

To their credit, most campus career centers go to great lengths to be crystal clear about the statistics they have gathered (and that they are sharing with current students). In their placement reports, they will feature explanations like the one above so that students (and others such as parents and legislators) know exactly what the numbers are and are not saying. On the other hand, some schools go to considerable lengths to blur or even conceal the real story behind the numbers. What is the situation at your school? Your healthy skepticism will help you find out.

In the meantime, see if your school's career center has a placement report that you can examine. If it does, you will undoubtedly uncover some helpful information there, particularly if you are trying to get a true sense of your job prospects where a major of interest is concerned. Just remember, though: Placement statistics are only as good as the data they are based upon—and what you learn from those statistics is only as good as your analysis of where the numbers came from in the first place.

Highlight This: See if your school's career center has statistics on the jobs landed by previous graduates of your institution. If it does, read them with a critical eye.

Your School's Alums Will Probably Help You—but Only If You Ask!

You might wonder why an alum would take time to help a total stranger who isn't even interested in the same field. It doesn't make sense until you sit on the other side of the desk. People who agree to serve as alumni contacts for their school do so because they genuinely want to help.

Rob Sullivan

As author and University of California-Santa Barbara graduate Jeff Gunhus writes in his book *No Parachute Required: Translating Your Passion into a Paycheck—and a Career* (Hyperion, 2001), your school's alumni tend to feel a certain "special connection" with the old alma mater—and thereby you:

> It still doesn't make any sense to me, but I love to talk to people who go to school at UC-Santa Barbara. It's fun to talk about the school and about the professors who are still there. I am more than willing to spend some extra time with UCSB graduates, simply because they are UCSB graduates. Is it an unfair advantage for me to give these people? Sure. But I want to find out what's going on in my old stomping grounds.

Most alums of any school feel exactly the same way. So if you contact them—with the help of your school's career center or alumni office—they will not only be willing to help you with your career, they will often be glad to do so.

For example, when career counselor Megan Meuli was a staff member at Hamline University in St. Paul, Minnesota, she met a student whose dream job was to work in film production. The student wanted to talk to someone working in the industry but was having no luck finding leads. So Megan turned to Hamline's online directory of alumni and found a 1991 alum who was working for E! Entertainment Television.

"I sent the alum an e-mail asking if the student could call or e-mail him to do an informational interview and learn about careers in TV production," says Meuli, now a career counselor at the University of Wisconsin-River Falls and in part-time private practice. "To both the student's and my surprise, the alum e-mailed back quickly to say yes."

That was not the end. Months later, the alum reconnected with Meuli to say he was going to be in the Twin Cities. Would any Hamline students be interested in chatting with him? Absolutely! A few faculty members showed up for the impromptu event as well—and one student left with an internship. "You just don't know what connections your school's alumni relations office or career center has," Meuli stresses.

It only makes sense: Often your school's alums have as much to gain from helping you as you have to gain from them. For starters, they know your school (and perhaps even your academic program as well), so you immediately have something in common with them. Additionally, most alums enjoy staying connected to their schools somehow, and advising you gives them a way to do that. ("So, what's going on at X University these days?" they might ask you.) Finally, many alums are looking for a way to give back to their schools without, or in addition to, giving money. Helping you is a way for them to do so in a very real, tangible way.

Of course, you too benefit from interacting with alums. Among other things, alums can teach you about the day-to-day realities of a particular field or company, make you aware of job openings (many of which may not be advertised through the usual channels), advise you on getting acclimated in a new city, or even help you pursue internships or other activities so that you can gain work experience before you graduate.

They will not be able to help you at all, though, unless you seek them out. Fortunately, locating and contacting alums from your school is easier than ever before. Thanks to campus offices like Career Services and Alumni Relations, as well as the Internet, there are many possibilities you can explore.

See If Your School's Career Center Sponsors a Formal Alumni Networking Program. Many college and university career centers have developed extensive programs through which alums have offered to be career resources to current students. At the College of St. Catherine in St. Paul, for instance, the Career Development Office's alumnae database features more than 2,000 St. Kate's alumnae who are willing to talk with current students about career issues in general as well as their own experiences in the world of work. Your school's career center may have a similar program that will help you locate and contact alums who can assist you.

Stop By Your School's Alumni Office (or Visit Its Web site) to Get a Copy of Its Alumni Magazine or Its Most Recent Alumni Directory. Most campus alumni offices publish a monthly or quarterly magazine that is sent to all alums who have contributed financially (or in some other way) to their alma mater. Often these magazines will list the names of alums who have recently donated something, describing what these men and women are now doing and where. Thus, you might be able to find an alum who graduated from your academic department three years ago so you can contact him or her for advice and guidance. At my own alma mater, for example, Minnesota State University Moorhead (MSUM), the quarterly *AlumNews* publication is freely available online at http://www.mnstate.edu/publications/alumnews. From there, you are literally one click away from the names and brief profiles of dozens of MSUM alums featured in each issue of the publication.

Similarly, many alumni offices publish an alumni directory (in print and/or online) listing contact information for hundreds or even thousands of alums. You might have to join your school's alumni association (yes, you can almost always do this even if you are still a current student) to get your hands on this publication. It will be well worth the small expense if it ultimately leads to an internship or a job, or even solid knowledge about a field or company of interest.

Check to See If There Are Any Branch Groups Affiliated with Your School's Alumni Office. Many alumni who move away from the city where they went to school organize alumni *chapters* in their new cities. Suppose, for example, that you are about to graduate from the University of Minnesota and you hope to move to the Denver, Colorado, area with your significant other. To get some job-related advice, you could get in touch with the Denver chapter of the University of Minnesota Alumni Association at http://www.umaa-denver.com and easily locate some Denver-based U of M alums you could talk to in person or via the phone or e-mail.

You can do something similar in reverse. If, for instance, you are originally from Portland, Oregon, and you are about to graduate from the University of Wisconsin-Madison, but you hope to return to Portland to find your first job, you could contact the Portland chapter of the University of Wisconsin Alumni Association at http://www.uwalumni.com/portland.

All of these alumni connection strategies take some work and diligence on your part, of course. You will undoubtedly run into alums who are not necessarily interested in giving you any of their time or energy, but in most cases, contacting alums is a wonderful investment of your time and energy. It is an often overlooked investment that will help you build your network, learn firsthand about the real world of work, and gather information that will lead you to satisfying career opportunities, both now and in the future.

And you just might make an alum's day at the same time.

Highlight This: Alums from your school often have a natural affinity for helping their fellow alums (and future alums). Take advantage of this phenomenon to learn about careers and organizations, as well as job and internship opportunities. Ask and ye shall (almost always) receive!

Look with Patience and an Open Mind

Speed Kills—This Won't Be Fast

Fast is fine, but accuracy is everything.

Xenophon

We have reached a point in our cultural development when you can do just about anything you want to *fast*. Need money? Stop by an ATM and pull some out of your bank account. Faster yet, just use a check card for your purchases. Want to hear your favorite song? Ninety-nine cents and a 30-second download later, it will be playing on your iPod. Need to talk to your friend who is studying abroad in England? Just call her—you both have cell phones, after all. Or, to save money, IM her or send her a quick e-mail. Assuming she is not busy on her side of the pond, you will probably hear back from her in minutes if not seconds.

As a fellow human being trying to manage a busy and complicated life, I share your love of near-instant access and the technology that invariably makes it so, but as a career counselor, the speed we have all become accustomed to drives me crazy. It makes it that much more difficult for me to deliver the bad news: career exploration and decision making ain't fast.

Now, don't get me wrong. If you have not done so already, you will run into tools and resources that can make career planning seem fast (or at least seem like it should be fast). Walk into practically any campus career center, for example, and you will likely be able to take a career assessment like the Strong Interest Inventory or the Campbell Interest and Skill Survey. Answer a couple hundred questions about your likes and dislikes and you will get pages of detailed results, usually featuring colorful charts and graphs that give the impression they could not possibly be inaccurate. But assessment results indeed can be inaccurate, at least in part. Worse, the assessment(s) you take—as its developer(s) and your career counselor will try to tell you—is meant only to *suggest* career possibilities, not *tell* you what career you "should" go into.

Your career center might also offer a computer-based career guidance system such as ACT Discover, SIGI-PLUS, or FOCUS. These programs allow you to input information about yourself and leave with information about majors and/or careers that might be a good fit for you. They have a definite put-in-some-data-and-I'll-spit-out-the-answers feel to them—sort of like a career development version of the voice-activated computers that Captain Kirk and Mr. Spock used years ago (or is that years *from* now?) on *Star Trek*. But like their print-assessment counterparts, these systems are meant only to suggest, not tell.

Even many of the career planning and job search books you see—with the exception, naturally, of the one you now hold in your hands—promise far more than they can or even should deliver where speed is concerned. I am sorry, but putting a decent résumé together takes us mere mortals more than one hour. Sure, you can write a résumé in an hour, but isn't the idea to write a *persuasive and compelling* résumé? Well, persuasive, compelling content takes time to develop. If you don't believe it, just ask any advertising professional who sweats for weeks or even months over a five-word campaign slogan or a half-page of radio advertising copy.

One of the most popular shows on television right now—especially among college students—is *CSI: Crime Scene Investigation*. Career services professionals at colleges and universities around the country are reporting a significant increase in the number of college students who say they would like to become crime scene investigators someday, a trend that is worrisome in the sense that there just are not that many crime scene investigators on the country's payrolls. But you know what I say to growing student fascination with crime scene investigation? Wonderful! Fantastic! In fact, let's enact legislation that compels every college student in America to take the types of courses that future detectives take. Why? Because then we would all come out of college with a detective mind-set that would encompass essential career skills like these:

Patience. Even on the more or less unrealistic one-hour crime shows on TV, you can see how patient the typical detective must be in order to succeed. Real-life detectives are either born or made patient. They go into every case assuming the going will be slow. If the case is quickly solved, that is a wonderful bonus. But slow is normal (if not always acceptable). Patience is also required when you are exploring career options. "Exploring," by its very definition, means looking around and seeing what you see.

Healthy Skepticism. Any good detective has a strong dose of healthy skepticism. When you are a detective, you simply do not automatically believe what someone is telling you, nor do you automatically believe that a crime scene is what it appears to be. Your default brain setting is, "I'll believe it when it's proven to me or confirmed." Until then, everything is open to change. If you were to switch your brain's default setting to "now wait a second" as you explore your career options, you would be much less likely to, for example, rule out careers that might fit you well, or rule in careers that will be disastrous for you.

Thoroughness. "Leave no stone unturned" goes the old cliché. For detectives, "leave no stone unturned" is a motto, a way of professional life. Good detectives look where no one else has looked and talk to people no one else has talked to. A waste of their time? Not at all. For if just one apparently "extra" step ultimately leads to solving the case, then the step was not really "extra" in the first place. If you are exploring a career in accounting, for instance, why not talk to four or five accountants instead of only one, so that you get a broader picture of the field from different perspectives? You may end up investing two or three or four extra hours of your time—but is that time really "wasted" if the result is a smarter career choice?

Willingness and Ability to Be Methodical. Every case is different, but detectives tend to go through a well-established investigative process in their work. They do not just jump in anywhere depending on how they feel or how much time they have or how many resources they have to work with. They follow a routine that is designed, in part, to make sure they "leave no stone unturned" (see "Thoroughness" above). Watch enough late-night, true-crime documentaries—the ones for which detectives are interviewed about difficult or fascinating cases they have handled—and you often hear the detectives talk about how their success in cracking the case stemmed in great part from their willingness and ability to be methodical about following their standard operating procedures.

In all my years of career counseling with college students and recent college grads, I can think of only a handful of clients who actually were willing and able to follow a process. If you are like many college students, for instance, you will want to race through or even skip self-assessment activities like the ones described earlier in Part I of this book. (Note: When I was in college, I did exactly the same thing—only to wish later that I hadn't.) You would rather simply get on with choosing a major or a career, in great part to get it over with (since anyplace is better than Limbo Land). Why not invest just a few hours—literally, just a few—in identifying your skills and abilities, interests, values, personality, and goals first, so that you make not just *a* decision but also an *informed* decision?

The Quest Mentality. Most detectives—especially the good ones—simply refuse to give up on a case. Years or even decades may pass and their day-to-day activities and priorities may change, but most detectives cannot let go of the unsolved crime until it is solved. They refuse to take no for an answer, not only for the sake of the victim's family and friends but also for their own satisfaction. They are determined to find the solution. This *quest mentality* will come in handy for you, too, especially as you explore career options. You probably can turn your seemingly competing interests in art and research into a career that actually pays the bills, but you will undoubtedly need to be persistent to pull it off.

Your need for speed as a college student is understandable and in some ways unavoidable. But it is also unattainable, at least where your career development is concerned. Detective work inevitably takes more time, energy, and money than you would prefer to spend. But the work still needs to be done if you want to crack the case that is your future career.

Highlight This: Like a good detective, the more methodical and patient you are in your career exploration and decision-making activities, the better the chance you will be successful—and satisfied—in the end.

You Can Make a Career Out of Almost Anything

> *It is not uncommon for me to talk to someone who tells me that they know precisely what they want to do and then they add, "But I couldn't possibly make any money doing that." Why are we so certain that love and money cannot coexist?*
>
> Barbara Winter

My friend Barbara Winter is a self-employment expert (and advocate) and author of the bestselling book *Making a Living Without a Job*. Published in 1993 (by Bantam), the book is in its 17th printing as I write this—so obviously Barbara did something right! It certainly explains why her seminars are so popular across the country and around the world.

Barbara has made a personal quest out of disproving the aggravating unsolicited advice thrown at practically everyone who explores off-the-beaten-path career options: "You could never make a living doing that." If you want to aggravate my friend Barbara Winter, use the word "can't" a lot—as in "I can't do this" or "I can't do that," or "You can't make a living doing that!" She will prove you wrong. Over the last 20-plus years, Barbara has learned that you almost always can find a way to "make a living doing that," whatever "that" might be. Indeed, Barbara can typically haul out an example or two—off the top of her head—of a person who is doing just fine, thank you, in a self-styled career. Among the people she might immediately cite:

- John Schroeder (http://www.gsfever.com), who has successfully combined his writing talents with his passion for garage sales to become both a book author (*Garage Sale Fever*, DeForest Press, 2005) and a nationally recognized authority on the subject (he has been interviewed by *Newsweek* and many other media outlets).

● Diane Grabowski and Jean Cheeley, who in their late forties took up motorcycling—at just about the same time they were both going through menopause. They ended up realizing that many of the experiences of learning to ride a motorcycle were comparable with various aspects of menopause. So they wrote a book, *Motorcycling Through Menopause* (Jorjeanna Press, 2003), which has spawned speaking opportunities they could not have imagined when they began their journey.

● Scott Rella, who has turned his love of ice sculpting into New York's oldest and most prestigious ice sculpting company, Ice Sculpture Designs (http://www.icesculpture-designs.com). Scott and his work have appeared on NBC's *Today* show and *Late Night with Conan O'Brien*, among other programs.

You don't have to be way beyond college age, however, to find—or create—an off-the-beaten-path career that combines the seemingly incompatible. Just ask 23-year-old Michael Casarella, a 2005 Hampshire College (Massachusetts) graduate who remembers the stress he was feeling late junior year as he contemplated how he could eventually make a living with a degree in literature and history.

"I have heard many a dejected liberal arts student describe themselves as 'over-educated and useless'—which I first classified as a sad but true statement in regards to myself," Casarella says. "I am a lover of literature and history; I enjoy studying older times and places, and imagining daily life and culture in great detail. I remember thinking that the only outlet I would have for this knowledge would be to write it, or teach it. I happen to have a great love for writing and practice it regularly, but I happen to know that it is work that is not always easy to come by, sometimes not sustainable, and does not always pay handsomely. So I was stressing quite heavily about my career and searching (in a doubtful way) for an alternative outlet for my passions."

He found that outlet in T-shirts—specifically, the front and back sides of T-shirts. For his senior thesis (a comprehensive project that all Hampshire students must design and complete in order to graduate), he studied 19th-century New York City and its most influential writers of the time. He took what he learned about the culture of the period and applied it to the T-shirt business that he and his brother had already begun to hatch over the previous summer. Today, Barking Irons (http://www.barkingirons. com) sells its one-of-a-kind T-shirts to 70 boutiques throughout the United States, not to mention stores like Barneys New York, Bloomingdale's, and Saks Fifth Avenue. The company has also been written up in the *New York Times* and many other media outlets—and one of its shirts was even worn by Brian Austin Green's character, Chris, on the ABC television sitcom *Freddie*.

"You should not assume that there is no place for your ideas," Casarella stresses. "You need to think creatively but keep a real-world mentality."

What it all boils down to is this: You can make a career out of almost any combination of skills and interests you can think of. If you can identify someone who is willing to pay you for it—whether that "someone" is an employer or a group of prospective customers—you can make a living doing it. Indeed, chances are someone else has already figured out a way to pull it off; you could do the same, either on your own or with the help of a counselor at your school's career center.

"Can't" is a powerful and deceiving word. It is the type of word that can stop you so cold that you do not even bother questioning its validity. So when you are exploring majors and careers, you are far better off adopting a philosophy of "perhaps I can" or "I can unless and until proven otherwise." You only need one job, after all. Just because it is not described in a book or listed on a Web site does not mean it doesn't exist—or couldn't.

Highlight This: You can probably make a career out of almost any activity you can think of—if you are creative and persistent enough to investigate the possibilities.

The Healthiest Attitude: 'I'm Not Lost; I'm *Exploring*!'

Not all who wander are lost.

J.R.R. Tolkien

Usually, I would not use the word "profound" to describe bumper sticker sayings. But several years ago, I did indeed stumble upon a bumper sticker phrase that struck me as quite insightful in the paradigm shift it implied. I was driving near the Minneapolis/St. Paul International Airport when I spotted the message, which said: I'm Not LOST; I'm EXPLORING!

It was good for a quick chuckle at the time. But not long after that, it began having a significant impact on me and the college students and recent graduates I work with in my career counseling practice, many of whom define themselves using such negative descriptors as "completely lost" and "clueless." I can relate. That is how I saw myself when I was in college and, especially, right after I graduated with my bachelor's degree in mass communications (journalism) in 1990. I did not know what I wanted or who might want me at the time. I managed to extend my sports-writing internship for almost a year following graduation, in hopes that buying time would buy me a clue. It didn't. So I made—or, more accurately, I was forced to make—one of the most demoralizing decisions of my young life: I moved back home with my parents. (Note to my parents: Nothing personal!)

I can still vividly recall the summer of 1991, even though my intuitive, big-picture personality typically prevents me from remembering yesterday or even an hour ago in much detail. I was not exploring at that time; I was lost, clueless. And that just made me depressed. (I did not see it this way at the time, but as I look back on the summer of '91 now, I am certain I could have been diagnosed as clinically depressed.) I felt like a total loser. And though my parents were incredibly supportive, in my mind I imagined their voices asking painful questions like "What's wrong with you?" and "Why can't you find a job?"

When you are in the "lost" frame of mind, you do not think about exploring; you do not see your situation as an opportunity. You just want to get "un-lost"—pronto. You will take the first decent job offer that comes along because anything is better than feeling like an idiot again tomorrow, and the next day, and the next. Indeed, you will run into this trap throughout college, especially early on during your freshman and sophomore years as you try to figure out what major to select and what career you will ultimately pursue. The pressure will come from two distinct sources:

- **Outsiders.** Your least favorite part of any vacation from school will be the annoying question you get from your parents, relatives, friends, and others: "So ... what are you majoring in?" Your "I don't know" or "I'm not sure yet" reply will bring not a pat on the back, but a look of puzzlement and perhaps even ridicule on each questioner's face. You will then return to school to find that every one of your friends (or so it seems) has everything figured out where majors and careers are concerned—leaving you as the only one (or so it seems) who is "completely lost" and "clueless."

- **Yourself.** "Why can't I figure this out?" you will admonish yourself. "What is wrong with me? Why am I the only one (or so it seems) who is so lost and clueless?"

There is only one problem with this hurry-up-and-choose tendency: The short-term "solution" of picking something—anything—just so you can get un-lost will only lead you deeper into the woods months or even years from now, when you will be even more lost than you are now. That is what happened to me. I was able to escape my parents' house four months after I got back there by taking a job at a small publishing company in Madison, Wisconsin. And while the job was not a bad one and I learned a lot in my time with the company, just shy of three years later I was lost again. I tried using the same sort of shortsighted strategy I used before to get un-lost: I went to graduate school to pursue my master's degree in journalism. It seemed sensible at the time—I was a journalist, after all—but I lasted only one semester before I realized I was just walking in circles.

Then—and only then—I finally did something right: I started looking around. "I'm not lost," I thought to myself (perhaps not in those exact words, but you get the idea); "I'm exploring!" Only then could—and did—I see that I did not need to limit myself to the world of writing and publishing. I had other skills and interests, and a desire to impact the world in other ways. Ironically, a master's degree in counseling became the path for me. (I say it is ironic because in journalism school they teach you *not* to get involved; in counseling school, they teach you *how* to get involved!)

On many campuses these days, there is no such thing as the "undeclared" or "undecided" major anymore. Instead, students who have not yet chosen a major are referred to as "open majors" (University of Iowa) or "exploratory majors" (University of Connecticut) or "deciding majors" (Xavier University of Louisiana) or _____. When you are defined in the negative—as in "undeclared" or "undecided"—you begin to see yourself in the negative and to be viewed by others in the negative. But if you are defined in the positive—as in "exploring" or "deciding"—you begin to see yourself in the positive and to be viewed by others in the positive.

Are you "lost" and "clueless" right now? Perhaps you should be "deciding" instead—seeing yourself not as someone lacking direction but as someone finding direction.

Highlight This: One person's "clueless" is another person's "deciding." The first descriptor suggests you are stuck; the second says you are moving. You are not lost; you are exploring!

Treat Career Exploration Like a Trip to the Toy Store—Look Around! Browse!

One doesn't discover new lands without consenting to lose sight of the shore for a very long time.

André Gide

Remember going to the toy store as a kid, when you were four or five or six years old? Perhaps you had five dollars in birthday money in your hand, just waiting to be spent. Or maybe you didn't have a penny to your name. It really didn't matter either way; you were at the toy store, and the toy store was absolutely full of the things you loved most: toys.

I can predict with near certainty how you proceeded from there. Even if your intent was to actually buy something, you probably did not walk directly to the shelf where that something was resting. Nope, you looked around. You no doubt started on the very first aisle, bobbing your head to the left and to the right and stopping frequently to take a closer look at whatever happened to catch your eye at that particular moment. If you had an adult with you, he or she might even have become impatient with your "dawdling." It didn't matter. For the real fun at the toy store was not in the *buying*; it was in the *looking*, the *browsing*.

By the time you left the toy store, perhaps you did indeed have a new toy in hand. But more importantly, you had new awareness of other toys—new toys you had not been previously aware of—that you would like to hold in your hot little hands someday.

Your browsing did not end when you were a youngster, though. Even as adults, we still like to look around. You may be someone who likes to page through new releases at the library or bookstore. You might enjoy trying on all of the season's new shoes to see if anything grabs your attention—or the attention of others. Heck, you might even look at stylebooks to get ideas about new ways to wear your hair. Browsing breeds possibilities.

But if you are like most people, you do not do any browsing where your career is concerned. You say you want to look at your options, but on a practical level you end up investigating only two or three careers (or academic majors) you are already familiar with, or that someone you trust has mentioned to you. Your intent is to explore—to really, truly explore—but your exploration does not really take you anywhere. You do not stumble upon anything new because you are really only looking at the old.

That is not exploration; that is limitation. And it is tragic—because a career or major that is great for you may be on the shelf two aisles down, and you will miss it if you do not walk around a bit.

Treat your career exploration the same way you treated your trip to the toy store. Take some time to browse. Yes, some people in your life—parents, relatives, advisers and other campus administrators—may eventually tell you to quit dawdling. But until then, take a genuine look around to see what you see. It is not terribly difficult or time-consuming to do. You can:

Page Through Career-Related Books at the Library, the Bookstore, or Your School's Career Center. Every year, dozens of publishing companies—including Ferguson, the publisher of the book you now hold in your hands—come out with new books on careers in various industries or careers for people who have various skills or traits. If you were to spend even 15 minutes paging through a few of these books, you would start to see just how many different ways there are to make a living in this world today.

Visit Web Sites That Describe Various Careers in Depth. One of the most vastly underused career resources is produced by the U.S. government's Bureau of Labor Statistics. It is called the *Occupational Outlook Handbook*, and it is updated every two years. (It is also freely available online at http://www.bls.gov/oco.) If you page through the printed version (available at practically all libraries, campus and public) or browse through the online version, you will quickly learn not only the titles of jobs you have never heard of, but also what those jobs are all about.

Use a Computer-Based Career Guidance System. Your school's career center probably offers one or more computer-based career guidance systems (e.g., ACT Discover, SIGI-PLUS, FOCUS). Some campus career centers even offer state-specific career guidance software. All of these programs feature listings of hundreds (if not thousands) of specific job titles, allowing you to easily get a better sense of what jobs are out there and how you might someday land one of them.

Ask People You Already Know to Tell You About Their Careers. The adults in your immediate life—family members, friends, acquaintances—have an assortment of jobs. So next time you get a ride home from your best friend's mother, for example, ask her informally about her career. What does she do each day? What does she like and not like about her job? How did she get into her line of work? Tell her you are simply curious, especially since you are at a point in life when you will be making some key career decisions. Mere curiosity coupled with a few key questions might open your eyes to a new career possibility before you are even out of the car.

Exploring career possibilities is not especially difficult (particularly if you ask for help from a campus career counselor or another trusted resource). But being on the ball enough to go ahead and actually do it is surprisingly rare, not only among college students but also among people in the general population. You browsed at the toy store as a kid. You browse elsewhere in your everyday life today. Browse for career possibilities, too. You can find treasures—but only if you go looking for them.

Highlight This: Use your natural human propensity to browse in your career exploration activities. Check out not only the careers you are already familiar with, but especially the ones you know little or nothing about. The career you have always dreamed about may be hiding on the shelf two aisles over.

When One Career Door Closes, Look for Others to Open

Opportunities are often things you haven't noticed the first time around.

Catherine Deneuve

Most everyone has a dream job. Mine, for example, is to be a professional golfer on the PGA tour, traveling around to exotic locales and competing for thousands of dollars every week. Heck, the year-round warm weather alone would make the job second to none in my mind. There is only one tiny little problem: I just do not have that kind of golf game, and I know it. When I was younger I was not bad, but even then my skills were nowhere near the level they would need to be to qualify for the PGA Tour, much less compete there.

Maybe you have come to a similar conclusion about your own dream job (though, hopefully, you have at least carefully thought it through first instead of simply dismissing it out of hand). The temptation for you at this point—and I wish I had an explanation as to why—will be to look in a completely different direction for a more "realistic" job. Stop! Please! Don't head off for new frontiers just yet. You might be able to live out your dream job in some other way, perhaps through a related job that is well within your grasp.

Have you ever played darts, even just casually? If you have, then you know that the idea is to aim for the bull's-eye, right? What happens when you inevitably miss the bull's-eye (far more often than you hit it, if you are anything like me)? Do you make a 180-degree spin and start throwing darts at the wall, or the TV, or the other people in the room? Of course not. You keep shooting for the bull's-eye, knowing that there are still valuable points to be earned for landing anywhere in its vicinity.

You should treat your career exploration—especially when it comes to your dream job—the very same way. Sadly, though, most college students who conclude that their dream job is out of reach start throwing "darts" all over creation—often puncturing themselves in the process—instead of continuing to take aim at careers that are in the vicinity of their dream job. Case in point: Steve (not his real name) was a student I worked with when I was a graduate student career counselor at the University of Wisconsin-Whitewater. He told me he was interested in a career in finance or accounting, but it was clear from his demeanor that he did not buy what he was telling me. So I asked him what career he would like to pursue if he thought he could—if there were no barriers standing in his way.

"That's easy," he said, in words I remember to this day. "I'd be a basketball writer for *Sports Illustrated*."

Turns out that Steve was a closet expert on NCAA basketball. None of his friends would participate in March Madness (the NCAA national basketball tournament, held annually in March) pools with him anymore because he predicted which teams would win with astonishing accuracy—the kind of expert foresight that costs others their money as well as their pride.

"So why," I asked Steve, "don't you try to become a basketball writer for *Sports Illustrated* someday?"

His troubling reply: "Oh, I could never do that."

And that was it—his sole reason for dumping his dream job was his own belief that he could "never do that." Now, that is tragic in and of itself (see **Question Your Sources as You Explore Career Options**, p. 91). But what I said to Steve next truly surprised him.

"Even if you can't or don't land a job as a basketball writer for *Sports Illustrated*, why couldn't you explore jobs that are similar to that one? Why have you abandoned the entire idea?"

I did not see my advice as particularly earth-shattering, but it was something that had never occurred to Steve. Perhaps, for example, he could be a basketball writer for some other publication. Or perhaps he could work for a basketball team. Or perhaps he could design the next revolutionary basketball shoe. Or perhaps he could make a difference in the lives of others by becoming a basketball coach. Or, well, you get the idea.

Steve knew what his bull's-eye career was. When he concluded it was out of reach, he started throwing darts all around the room, puncturing himself in the process. Only when I suggested that he could continue shooting around the target did he begin to see other viable career possibilities. You can—and indeed should—use this same strategy in your own career exploration. Suppose, for example, that your dream job is to be a pop singer but you conclude, after much exploration and deliberation, that you are just not going to be appearing on the cover of *Rolling Stone* anytime soon. Is there any way you could find some other satisfying career in the world of pop music or music in general? Absolutely! Consider these possibilities:

- If you are good with your hands, maybe you could pursue a career designing or building musical instruments.

- If you have an investigative, analytical sort of mind, perhaps you would enjoy studying music and its effects on, say, intelligence or memory.

- If you are a true artistic type, maybe you would like writing about music for a magazine or composing music for children's videos.

- If you are a helper type, perhaps you would get a kick out of working as a music therapist, using music and musical instruments to help people work through their physical and/or psychological issues.

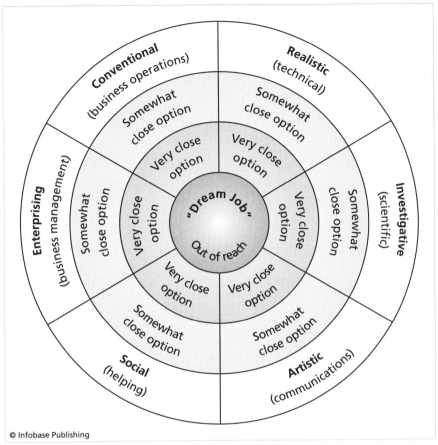

© Infobase Publishing

If your dream job is out of reach, try shooting for a closely related job.

- If you are into business, maybe you would be happy working in or owning a music store, or heading up a local arts organization.

- If you are into structure and routine, perhaps you could see yourself working as an accountant for a music publishing company, or as a financial planner for a commercially successful musician.

There is almost always a way to do something related to your dream job, even when your dream job is (or seems to be) out of reach. Sometimes you just have to think about pursuing your dream job in a different setting, location, or sector of the economy. Sometimes you just have to think about pursuing your dream job in a different way than you had originally hoped or planned.

Whatever the case, there is no need for you to arbitrarily and prematurely slam the door completely on your dream. Indeed, you just may find, as many others have, that when one career door closes on you, many others open, or could open, leaving you in a position to throw your darts at satisfying options you never would have considered before.

Highlight This: Even if you cannot hit the bull's-eye that is your dream job, you can find a satisfying career close to that target.

PART II

BE CAREFUL OF WHAT YOU THINK YOU KNOW!

Introduction

Think About
How You Think

Education is learning what you didn't even know you didn't know.

Daniel Boorstin

I had a revealing phone conversation a while back with an undergraduate student from the University of Wisconsin-Whitewater, the school where I earned my master's degree in counseling.

I knew why the student was calling. She was volunteering for the annual alumni fundraising phone-a-thon, and she was going to hit me up for, er, ask me to donate money. But as the student and I traded small talk about how things were going at good ol' UW-Whitewater, she asked me what my major was while I was there.

"Counseling," I replied. "I was in the master's program. But as an undergraduate I was a journalism major."

"You can do that?" was the student's incredulous response.

"Do what?" I asked, not knowing what she meant.

"Well, I'm a communications major—I'm in public relations—and I've always thought about going into counseling or something like that," the student said. "I just didn't think I had the right background for it."

"What's the right background?" I asked, quickly putting on my counselor's "hat."

"I don't know—maybe there is no right background," the student concluded.

After assuring the student that her background sounded just fine for a helping field, and encouraging her to visit with one of my old professors in the counseling program, I wished her luck and hung up the phone—50 bucks poorer but left with yet another example of how our beliefs, assumptions, and perceptions play such a critical role in our choices of college majors and careers.

How many times have you heard statements like these, or made them yourself?

- "I would like to go into teaching, but my dad says there is no money in it."

- "Sure, it would be fun to major in art—but I will never get a job in it. Everybody knows that."

- "My roommate told me that all computer programmers do is sit behind a computer all day long and write code."

Have you ever thought about where these conclusions come from? As I have seen in my work with college students, my research on students' career decision making, and even in my own life, more often than not these perceptions rely on shaky evidence at best and downright falsehoods at worst. Yet they can carry enormous weight in your career decision making, so much so that you might fail to explore certain career options or, perhaps more tragically, prematurely conclude that certain career dreams are simply out of reach.

College, in a nutshell, is all about *critical thinking*—questioning and challenging the "known" and learning to be open to the unknown. Nowhere is critical thinking more important than in your investigation of college majors and careers. So as you explore:

Never Assume. Do not assume that you—or, just as importantly, other people who are close to you—already know everything about a major or career you are considering. You likely know only a fraction of what there is to know; you probably have to go out and find the rest.

Gather Information from Many Sources. If you are thinking about a particular major, do not just ask your roommate about it.

Talk to professors in the department. Go to your school's career center and discuss the major with a counselor. (Many career centers have "What Can I Do with a Major in ... ?" handouts available in print form or on their Web sites.) Ask the career center if there are any alums who pursued the major you are considering and who would be willing to talk with you about what they did with it.

Critically Evaluate Your Sources. Think carefully about where you are getting your information on majors and careers. How do your parents, friends, and roommates, for example, *really* compare with the U.S. Department of Labor when it comes to knowing trends in various industries? Who will *really* be able to give you a better sense of what it is like to be a professional dancer—a dance professor, or your assigned faculty adviser from the chemistry department?

Test Your Ideas. Most campuses offer many opportunities to try out career paths. If you are thinking about becoming a financial planner, for example, see if your school's career center offers a *job shadowing* or *externship* program through which you can spend a day or two with a working financial planner. That way you can see firsthand the pros and cons of working in that particular field. Similarly, check to see whether your campus offers semester-long or yearlong internship or co-op programs, which will give you an even more extensive look at a particular field.

Challenging your own beliefs, assumptions, and perceptions about college majors and careers takes time and effort to be sure. Clearly you will be making an investment—but it is an investment that could mean the difference between the discouragement of "the road not taken" and a satisfying future career.

Let's take a look at some key career issues you should think critically about during your college years.

Confront Your Internal Beliefs

Think 'What Will I Do First?' Instead of 'What Will I Do with My Life?'

It is a mistake to look too far ahead. Only one link in the chain of destiny can be handled at a time.

Sir Winston Churchill

Take a moment to reflect back upon the last five years of your life. Think about all the changes you have gone through in that time. Perhaps you finished high school and started college. Or perhaps you returned to college after spending some time in the workforce, in the military, or in a full-time parenting role. You have gained new skills over the last five years, not to mention new interests. And at least some of your values have changed as well—perhaps subtly, perhaps profoundly.

You are just not the same person today that you were five years ago.

Now take a minute to think about how the world around you has evolved (or devolved, depending on your point of view) over the past five years. Technology, for instance, has expanded ever further. Today's lexicon includes terms like *podcasting* and *blogging* and *HDTV*. Heaven only knows what tomorrow will bring. In the meantime, life-altering events have pounded into us the reality that as much as we want to control our environment, in many ways we are subject to its whims, be they man-made or flukes of nature.

Our world is just not the same today as it was five years ago.

You will continue to change throughout the rest of your life. The world will too. That is why it is impossible—not to mention unwise—for you to frame your career decision-making activities using pressure-packed questions like these:

- What will I do with my life?

- What should I be when I grow up?

- Where do I see myself 40 years from now?

Take the first concept, for example: "What will I do with my life?" According to U.S. Bureau of Labor Statistics data released in 2004, the average person who was born near the tail end of America's baby boom generation held 10 different jobs between the ages of 18 and 38. Chances are you will hold even more jobs in that time given the drastically different nature of today's economy and job market. Meanwhile, anecdotal evidence suggests that you will change careers completely three or four times. Perhaps your grandfather worked for one company for 45 years and retired from the organization with a gold watch and a going-away party. Your father and mother probably chuckle at this notion now as they go through their own working lives, wondering whether they will want to be doing the same thing five years from now and whether their employers—not to mention their jobs—will still be around at that time.

What should you be "when you grow up"? That idea just does not make sense anymore. For starters, the question goes right back to mistakenly implying that you will have one and only one job or career throughout the 40 or so years you will be working. Even more problematic, though, is this question's mistaken assumption that there is a magical age or developmental level when you will become—and be seen as—a "grown-up" who is, well, finished growing. But no matter what your age, you are never static; you are constantly developing and changing. It is not as though you someday reach a point where you are fully baked—when you are "done."

Where do you see yourself 40 years from now? Most of us do not know where we will be 40 hours from now or even 40 minutes from now! Perhaps you are in your twenties as you read this book. Is your life as a twentysomething fully aligned with the picture you had of that life when you were, say, five?

I raise all of these seemingly ridiculous questions to make a serious point: Attempting to figure out now what your entire life's career path will (or should) be is an exercise in futility. It is also completely unnecessary. Unless you are the incredibly rare exception to today's rule, you will not do any one thing for your entire working life. You will be doing several things—and there is a good chance you have no clue right now what the middle and latter parts of your working life will look like.

As I write this, I am 38 years old—soon to be 39. I was 23 when I graduated from college in 1990 and began wrestling with the hopelessly overwhelming "what will I do with my life" question. All it got me was self-inflicted despair and confusion. Think about it. In 1990 the Internet was in existence only among a select few university and government nerds. Phones still had cords attached to them, and they were still landlines. We were only starting to understand what desktop publishing programs could do to help us create cool brochures or newsletters—all of which would ulti-mately be printed in hard copies, of course. And we were just beginning to see the globalization of the world—sometimes for better, other times for worse.

With all of that and much more unfolding, did I really have a realistic chance of pinpointing—right then and there—what I would, could, or should be pursuing as a career for my entire life? Of course not. Your situation today is no different. If anything, you have even less of a chance of identifying an entire life's work right now; the world is changing faster than ever, and you are changing right along with it.

So it makes no sense at all for you to think in terms of "what should I do with my life?" you are far better off instead thinking in terms of "what will my *first* job or career after college be?" or "what will I do *next*?" Making career decisions carries enough pressure as it is. Why add to that pressure unnecessarily by framing those decisions in unrealistic terms like "the rest of my life"?

I wish I had known in 1990 that I could make my career decisions about 2015 in 2015. You can—and should—do the same.

Highlight This: Unless you can predict the future, yours and that of the world around you, it is both impossible and unnecessary to choose a career that will last your entire working lifetime. Think instead of what you will do first or next.

Question Your Sources as You Explore Career Options

Ask a question and you're a fool for three minutes; do not ask a question and you're a fool for the rest of your life.

Chinese proverb

Suppose you are in the market for an inexpensive used car and you run into me, the proud owner of a 1994 Nissan Sentra with nearly 200,000 miles on it (which is actually true, by the way). "It's a great runner," I tell you, "and I have taken very good care of it over the years. I have changed the oil faithfully every 3,000 miles, and I have followed the owner's manual to the letter when it comes to taking the car in for its scheduled maintenance. It gets close to 40 miles a gallon on the highway, it has very little rust, and all of the major components are in good working condition. The only reason I am selling it is because it's really just too small for me." (I am 6 feet, 4 inches tall.)

I am asking $1,100 for the car. "That is its blue-book value," I say. So you hand over your $1,100 immediately and buy the car, right?

Of course not! You are not even close to making a decision yet. Instead you will undoubtedly:

Ask to Take the Car for a Test Drive. You will want to spend a half hour or more taking the car through its paces, both on the city streets and on the highway. Does the car shimmy once you go beyond 50 miles per hour? Do the brakes feel good? Does the car make strange or annoying sounds as it is going down the road?

Take the Car to a Mechanic You Trust. For $50, your professional-mechanic friend will inspect any car you bring to him, from bow to stern, top to bottom. He will look for flaws major and minor—particularly dangerous leaks, loose connections, and anything else that might spell disaster down the road (literally and figuratively).

Call Your Friend, the Owner of a '96 Sentra. One of your close friends from high school drives a slightly newer Sentra. You want to talk to her to find out what kind of luck she has had with it, what major repairs she has had to make and at what cost, and whether she would buy another Sentra again or not.

Go Online to Research the Car. You will jump on the Internet to first check out the car's book value according to several sources. Then you will do a Google search to find a few online user groups made up of people who have firsthand experience—both good and bad—with Sentras. You decide to post a question seeking opinions about the purchase you have in mind.

You may even go so far as to ask a reference librarian to help you find articles about the car. You are aware that several magazines publish annual features on the best used cars to buy. You want to see if the Sentra showed up in any of those articles.

In other words, no matter how honest and knowledgeable I might seem where my '94 Nissan Sentra is concerned, you know better than to take me at my word about the car, for I may well be dishonest about it, unknowledgeable about it, or both. You have no way of knowing one way or the other, and you would be stupid to risk it given the fact that you will be spending $1,100 of your hard-earned cash just to buy the car, to say nothing of the money you will have to invest to maintain it in the years to come.

Common sense tells you that you just do not buy a used car based solely on the claims of its owner, even if that owner is completely honest (like me). Instead, you go to outside people and resources first to see if the owner's claims mesh with reality. Like a good journalist, you check out your source—me, in this case—and make sure he is reliable and accurate before you go and drop $1,100 on his car.

Sadly, too many college students—I was one of them—misplace this same type of common sense when they are exploring college majors and careers. All it takes sometimes is one snide comment from a roommate or the friend of a friend to convince you that your career idea is hopelessly ridiculous. The conversation might go something like this:

> **You:** I'm thinking of majoring in anthropology.
> **Roommate:** Are you crazy? You will never get a job with that!
> **You:** Hmmm … maybe I should major in something else, then.

If you are like most college students, you never stop to consider that your roommate knows as much about anthropology and the anthropological job market as a paper towel does. He sounds like he is an expert; why would he be so vocal with his opinion, after all? So he must be worth listening to. And so, sadly, you do listen, and you take your career exploration elsewhere.

The media, television and movies in particular, can have this same type of impact on your career exploration activities. In 2005, NBC *Tonight Show* host Jay Leno was taken to task by Betty Young, the president of Northwest State Community College in Ohio, who was tired of hearing the late-night comedian's less-than-flattering jokes about the academic rigor of community colleges and the abilities of community college students. She was concerned enough to ride her Harley-Davidson to Los Angeles in an attempt to meet with Leno personally. Being joked about in front of a national television audience is enough to make any student reconsider his or her plan to pursue a degree of some sort at a two-year institution, notwithstanding the fact that many graduates of community and technical colleges find careers that are quite satisfying.

So as you explore majors and careers, challenge the sources of your information, especially the people sources. Who, for example, is really the most knowledgeable person when it comes to career possibilities with an anthropology degree: your roommate, or a regional officer of the American Anthropological Association? What is the best way for you to get an accurate picture of a career in crime scene investigation: watching *CSI: Miami*, or talking to a local crime scene investigator who has worked in the field for 20 years?

You need not travel thousands of miles on a motorcycle to ask the kinds of tough questions that will help you choose the right road.

Highlight This: Your sources of career information—especially the people sources—may or may not be accurate and reliable. Treat them all with healthy skepticism.

Do Not Let Old Assumptions Keep You from Newfound Happiness

Often we think we can't only because we haven't made the effort to research how we could.

Laurence Boldt

In 1996, I witnessed the tragedy that ultimately drove me to become a career counselor.

I was a graduate student at the University of Wisconsin-Whitewater, studying to become a counselor. I had volunteered to lead a career-planning group made up of freshmen and sophomores who were still trying to figure out what to major in and what career to pursue after graduation. They were among the school's many "undecided" students—at least, they were *supposed* to be "undecided."

During the first meeting of the first career-planning group I ever led—and during that night's first icebreaker activity—I had a 30-second interaction with a student that ended up having a profound impact on me. The activity was straightforward enough: The students were to pair up with partners and tell each other one of their interests. It was just a way to help the participants get to know each other, nothing more. There were an odd number of participants that night, and I noticed that one student ended up by herself. So I took it upon myself to be her partner for the activity. I walked up to her, introduced myself, and casually asked her, "What's something you're interested in?" I cannot honestly say I remember her response verbatim, but what follows is very close: "I'm not sure why I'm even here in this group; I know what I want to do as a career. I want to do something with my artwork. But you can't make a living doing that."

I was not on the ball enough at the time to ask her why she felt this way. I just shrugged and told her about one of my interests. (Stupid, Pete, stupid.) Only later, as I was walking back to my car, did it dawn on me that this student's conclusion was decidedly inaccurate. "There *are* jobs in art," I thought to myself. "I work with a graphic artist practically every day. And somebody is creating all the posters I see, and all those ads in the magazines I read, and all those paintings on the greeting cards I buy."

Somehow, this student had bought into the idea that she could not possibly get a job in the field that was already of high interest to her. She was not "undecided" at all; she knew what she *wanted* to do where her career was concerned. But she had ruled that option out completely—to the degree that she did not even question whether her "no jobs in art" assumption was correct or not.

That is the tragedy of which I speak. Here was a student who already had a vision of her future but who had pushed it aside because of, well, because of who knows what. Without questions and without a fight, this student had given up on her quite achievable dream.

This phenomenon became the subject of my master's thesis, for which I interviewed nine "undecided" undergraduates to learn more about their thinking where academic majors and careers were concerned. That is when I ran into Jim (not his real name), who unknowingly reminded me of why I had chosen my topic. When I asked him to temporarily set aside any perceived barriers he saw and then choose a career he would like to pursue, his response was immediate and clear: He said he would like to be a teacher. But to him, that was an impossibility.

"Why?" I asked incredulously.

"Well, I guess I just sort of *assumed* [emphasis added] I couldn't do it," he replied.

Finally, someone had—albeit unknowingly—put a word to the phenomenon I kept seeing over and over again in the undecided students I was working with: *assume*. Many so-called "undecided" students, I concluded, were not "undecided" at all when it came to identifying careers they *wanted* to pursue. They just assumed—for some reason(s)—that those careers were hopelessly out of reach. And instead of questioning those assumptions, they had simply moved on.

Do not make this mistake yourself! If you have ruled out a certain major or career—or if you are about to—step back for a minute (preferably longer) and ask yourself if the conclusions you have reached are based on assumptions (bad) versus solid information (good). Where did your conclusions come from? Who or what has influenced them? Are these influences reliable and accurate?

Wouldn't it be a shame—a tragedy—if you were to pass up a major or a career for shaky reasons at best or downright falsehoods at worst? Perhaps you already do have a major or career you would like to pursue but you have concluded it is out of reach. How do you know it is out of reach? What if it is not?

Highlight This: If you do not question your assumptions, beliefs, and perceptions, you will be prone to ruling out wonderful career possibilities prematurely and unnecessarily.

Beware of Either/Or Thinking

When one door of happiness closes, another opens;
but often we look so long at the closed door that we
do not see the one which has been opened for us.

Helen Keller

I once worked with a college student who had an overwhelming love of animals—a passion that only made the career conclusions she had reached that much more painful for her.

Shannon (not her real name) did not have the greatest of grades, but in her mind that was only a tiny part of a much bigger, and insurmountable, problem: She could not be a veterinarian. She did not have the stomach for it, for starters, as she had discovered during a two-day job shadowing experience she'd had with a veterinarian the summer before. Moreover, she said, her incredibly shy demeanor (and she definitely was quiet) would never allow her to interact with pet owners in the way she envisioned as being "normal" among professionals in the field.

These conclusions were troubling enough as far as I was concerned. After all, Shannon was making broad generalizations based on limited evidence at best. But the kicker, as it turns out, was even worse: The reason Shannon was so despondent was only tangentially related to the idea that she could not become a veterinarian. More troublingly, she had come to believe that she would not be able to work with animals *at all*, in any career, because—in her mind, at least—the only people who make a living working with animals are veterinarians.

Another student I worked with (see the story of Brian in **Internship Is Just One Name for Valuable Experience**, p. 140) had an extensive background in Spanish. Among other things, he had trained the Spanish-speaking employees at the restaurant where he worked, and he had co-taught English as a Second Language (ESL) classes at a nearby technical college. Indeed, he enjoyed teaching and training activities so much that he wanted to become a teacher after he graduated. But by the time he came to see me, he had decided he could not become a teacher. Why? Because he had not taken the courses necessary to obtain his teaching license, which would have qualified him for a job as a high school Spanish instructor.

Both Shannon and Brian had fallen into the trap of *either/or* thinking where their career decision making was concerned. It is a danger you, too, will face as you identify career possibilities and then make decisions about which ones to explore in depth. If you are not careful, the either/or trap will snare you too, often when you could have easily dodged it.

Take Shannon, for example. Perhaps you know someone like her; perhaps you *are* her. Shannon made the colossal but all too common mistake of buying into the notion that if you want to work with animals, *either* you must be a veterinarian *or* you must find some other career. She had not even considered the idea that there might be other possibilities to explore. For example, I was at one of the local public libraries a couple of years ago when I noticed quite the ruckus coming from the children's section, which was on the other side of the building from where I was sitting. Curious, I walked over to take a look. There I saw a large group of kids—two- and three-year-olds, perhaps—who were sitting on the floor, legs crossed and in absolute awe of the woman standing before them: an educator from the Minnesota Zoo who was holding on her arm a parrot of some sort. Her job was teaching the kids about parrots and the other animals she had brought with her for the show.

Every month, my four-year-old son gets his very own copy of *Ranger Rick* magazine. The thing is filled with pictures and stories about animals of every sort. Someone—more than one person, actually—puts that publication together every 30 days or so. Shannon could be, or could have been, one of those people.

And what about Brian? To him, *either* you were a school teacher *or* you were not a teacher at all. Once he and I talked for a while, he began to see that a high school classroom is just one place where you can be a teacher. You may not be called a "teacher" in, say, a corporate setting where you are preparing customer service reps to better serve Spanish-speaking clients; you will probably be called a "trainer" instead. But you are still as much a teacher as is someone educating 16-year-olds in a high school classroom.

So if you are passionate about a certain something—whether it is fashion or cars or coffee—give yourself the chance to see just how many different careers exist around that topic. Perhaps you cannot or do not want to be a fashion *designer*, for instance. But that does not mean you cannot become a fashion *writer*, or a fashion *buyer*, or a fashion *publicist*. Similarly, do not feel obligated to choose between two areas of strong interest—*either* this *or* that. If you like both sports and art, for example, perhaps you could become a sports caricaturist, or a sports poster designer, or a sports illustrator for a magazine. It is not always necessary—or wise—to take one passion and leave the other.

Beware of either/or thinking when it comes to your career exploration and decision-making activities. Save either/or for your intermediate algebra class—where your conclusions really are *either* right *or* wrong. The world of careers is not black and white; it is gray.

Highlight This: Your career choices will not be—and do not need to be—either/or decisions. If one particular career path is not going to work for you (for whatever reason), chances are you can find several others to investigate.

Career Decision-Making Traps to Avoid

Begin challenging your own assumptions.
Your assumptions are your windows on the world.
Scrub them off every once in a while, or the light won't come in.

Alan Alda

I am always amazed by the haphazard, less-than-fully-informed way most college students make their career-related decisions. Then again, perhaps I should not be surprised, because I subscribed to the exact same approach when I was in college.

When I arrived at Moorhead State University in the fall of 1985, I had already declared a major: mathematics. But really, my mother was the one who had steered me into math. And it made sense, to both of us, at the time. I was pretty good at math, and the scuttlebutt (according to my high school guidance counselor) was that the country would really need more math teachers by the time I would graduate four (well, it was supposed to be four) years later.

Neither my mother nor my father pressured me to become a math major. It was merely the option that seemed most logical; it was the path of least resistance. So I took it.

Two and a half years later, when I had finally figured out that I really did not enjoy mathematics very much, and I really was not all that great at it when we got to the more complex stuff, I decided to change majors. I enjoyed writing—I still do—so I opted for mass communications. Literally, it was that fast and that simplistic. It took me longer to type the last sentence than it did for me to adopt mass communications as my new academic home. I had already ruled out the majors my friends had picked: political science, chemistry, and English among them. I never bothered to explore the dozens of other majors offered at Moorhead State. (I could have been a great psychology major, if only I had known that such a field existed.) And the future job market for mass communications majors? The thought never even crossed my mind until, well, an hour after graduation day in May 1990.

I never did feel completely comfortable with my mass communications choice, but I could never put my finger on why. I was not truly satisfied in my first real postgraduation job (in publishing) either, and again, I could never pinpoint the reasons. But there was always a sort of vague malady of fear and dissatisfaction behind what I was doing, both during college and in the years immediately after. I just could not diagnose its causes. Where had I gone wrong?

I am starting to figure it out—and you can do the same—thanks to my new awareness of the specific career decision-making mistakes we are all prone to making. They are outlined clearly in a source you may see as an unlikely one: the book *Should You Really Be a Lawyer?* (Decision Books, 2005), by Deborah Schneider and Gary Belsky. Schneider and Belsky borrow concepts from a field called *behavioral economics*—essentially, the study of how people make judgments and decisions involving money—to explain how various decision-making "traps" can (and often do) have a significant impact on the career-related choices we make. Until I read this book—and learned even more by interviewing Deborah Schneider for an article—I had no clue that the career decision-making quandaries I once wrestled with have names. Name a problem and there is a good chance you can address it and ultimately fix it.

Do any of the following career decision-making traps—or *choice challenges*, as Schneider and Belsky like to call them—sound familiar to you?

Anchoring—Attaching yourself so firmly to an idea that you do not bother to even think about exploring other possibilities.

Example: You are going to become a teacher because, well, you have always pictured yourself as a teacher.

Confirmation Bias—Seeking out only information that supports your current line of thinking (and ignoring information that contradicts it).

Example: You quit talking to your older brother—who is encouraging you to major in your passion, art—and instead talk careers with your fellow finance majors and your favorite finance professor.

Decision Paralysis—Being so overwhelmed with possibilities that you decide not to choose any of them; you decide not to decide!

Example: You are interested in majoring in psychology, or sociology, or public relations, or graphic design, or marketing. "Forget it," you conclude, "I will just stay undeclared."

The Herd Mentality—Making decisions based on what the people around you are doing.

Example: All your friends are majoring in accounting, so you figure you will do the same.

Ignoring the Base Rate—Disregarding the odds, the *base rate*, in a particular situation.

Example: Deciding you will pursue a career as a professional football player even though a mere handful of athletes have the ability to play at that level.

Example: Opting against majoring in art history because there are "no jobs" in that field (even though the reality is that there are indeed some jobs in that field).

The Information Cascade—Being so barraged by a particular idea that you start to believe it completely—and make decisions based upon it.

Example: "I am not going to major in computer science. All the IT jobs these days are going overseas."

Mental Accounting—Treating money in different ways depending on where it comes from or what you are spending it on.
Example: "I don't really want to go to med school, but what the heck—Grandpa is paying for it."

Regret Aversion—Making decisions based on your fear of feeling bad in the future.
Example: Your heart is not really into studying abroad, but you are afraid that if you do not do it you will kick yourself later in life.

The Status Quo Bias—Preferring to stay with the known for fear that the unknown will be worse.
Example: Sure, you cannot stand your mathematics major, but at least you know what you are up against. God only knows what another major would be like.

The Sunk Cost Fallacy—Not wanting to "waste" the time, energy, or money you have already invested in something.
Example: "I do not like law school, but I am already two years and thousands of dollars in. I have to finish now."

Do you see yourself ensnared in any of these career decision-making traps? Then it is time to break free, either on your own or, better yet, with the help of a counselor or adviser at your school's career center. Once you have escaped the misguided conclusions that are clogging your mind, you will be able to make the informed choices that will ultimately lead to career satisfaction and success.

Highlight This: The mental shortcuts you take have a profound influence on the career choices you make—for better or for worse.

Confront Your External Influences

Geography Matters in Your Career Decision Making

*The more you put yourself in the way of opportunity,
the better your chances of getting what you want.*

Ron LeGrand

True or false: A college student who majors in accounting has better postgraduation job prospects than does a student who majors in art history.

False. False, that is, if the accounting major goes back to live in his hometown of 452 people while the art history major moves to, say, New York City or Washington, D.C., where art-related jobs are comparatively plentiful.

True, accounting majors typically have an easier time finding a job than art history majors do. But as soon as you leap to the generalization that this statement is always true, you fall prey to spreading—and worse, buying into—a falsehood. Sadly, it is the type of misguided belief that could easily dissuade you from pursuing a major and/or a career that would have been a great fit for you. Conversely, it could mistakenly convince you that the major or career you have chosen is a sure bet when it is really not.

Ask any music major, or religious studies major, or psychology major, or practically any other liberal arts major what the typical reaction is when she tells people what she is majoring in and you will likely hear stories of discouraging comments like these:

- "You are majoring in _____ [insert liberal arts major of your choice here]? What are you going to do with that?"

- "You will never get a job with a _____ [insert liberal arts major of your choice here] major."

- "You are kidding, right? Why don't you major in something marketable, like _____ [insert "practical" major of your choice here]?"

Everyone, it seems, has an opinion where your chosen major or career path is concerned. Far more often than not, that opinion is uninformed at best and flat-out wrong at worst—especially when you take geography into account. The person who tells you, for example, that your psychology degree "isn't marketable" has no clue how many thousands of Americans with psychology degrees are happily employed in the world of work—usually in large, urban areas where there are simply more diverse opportunities to pursue (and where thousands of other former liberal arts majors—who are now employers—know firsthand the value of a liberal arts background).

Similarly, ask any finance major, or computer science major, or accounting major, or practically any other business-school major what the typical reaction is when she tells people what she is majoring in and you will likely hear stories of gushing comments like these:

- "Smart. Very smart."

- "You will have a job in no time."

- "You are golden."

That student will soon believe she has made an outstanding choice. But she may start changing her tune when she decides she cannot or will not leave the rural area where she grew up, where job openings of any kind are relatively rare.

Geography matters in your career decision making, as many once-worried college students have been pleased to discover after finding the right place to pursue their dreams—and as many other once-confident students have been shocked to learn after finding out that their shoo-in major or career choice was not such a sure thing after all. The career you choose means little if you do not also consider where you will be pursuing it—or trying to, as the case may be.

Highlight This: You cannot accurately judge your chances of landing a job in a particular field unless and until you take into account where—geographically speaking—you will be looking for that job. The job that is practically impossible to find in Rome, Georgia, might be quite popular in Rome, Italy.

Labor Market Forecasts—
Handle with Care

*The only relevant test of the validity of a hypothesis is
comparison of prediction with experience.*

Milton Friedman

Remember the good old 1990s—1998 and 1999, to be exact?
The American economy was flying high, thanks in great part to
the emergence and astounding growth of technology companies
that were rich with both ideas and venture capital. Brand-new
college graduates with technology-related degrees were waltzing
into jobs with high salaries, and dot-com companies were offering
borderline-ridiculous perks: everything from gym memberships
and company cars to on-site game rooms where you could play
air hockey over lunch. The good times were definitely rolling, and
there seemed to be no end in sight.

Many of the students starting college at that time heard and
read about this delightful scene and, understandably perhaps,
signed up for technology majors themselves, thinking they too
would like a piece of the action four years hence. But a funny
thing happened on the way to utopia: the dot-com bubble burst,
and by the time the freshmen of 1998 and 1999 graduated in
2002 or 2003, the lucrative jobs with perks like office Ping-Pong
tables thrown in—the ones that were supposed to be waiting for
them—were long gone.

The unfortunate result: thousands of disappointed and dis-
enchanted new college grads, many of whom were not particularly interested in technology careers in the first place. I heard

from them often on MonsterTRAK's Career Planning for College Students message board (which I oversee), sharing their disappointment with a combination of venom, frustration, and self-flagellation. Their collective question: "Where are all these IT jobs everyone was telling us about four years ago?"

If you read enough newspaper and magazine articles or watch enough television news programs, you will invariably see stories about the career fields that are "hot" today and the ones that will be "hot" tomorrow. The information is presented as though it is a foregone conclusion. But as thousands of IT grads from the Classes of 2002 and 2003 will quickly tell you, "tomorrow" involves predictions, not facts.

Government agencies like the U.S. Department of Labor's Bureau of Labor Statistics go to elaborate scientific lengths to forecast which occupations will see high employment demand in the years immediately ahead. They look at census data, information provided by organizations and employers, history, and all sorts of other factors to make the best predictions they can about what the world of work will look like two, five, ten, even twenty or more years down the road. Sometimes their forecasts are close to perfect. Other times they are anything but perfect. And you have no way of knowing which is which when you are trying to decide on a career path.

That is why it is so dangerous for you to make your academic and career decisions based solely on labor market forecasts. Those seemingly solid predictions may turn out to be dead wrong by the time you finish college. You will be left looking for a job in a much smaller pool of possibilities. Worse, the extra motivation and dedication you will need to succeed in that type of scenario will not be forthcoming—because your heart or your skills may not have been in your chosen field to begin with.

Part of the problem for IT grads from the classes of 2002 and 2003 was the fact that they were all competing for far fewer total jobs than they thought would be available after they graduated. But many of them did not feel like competing for jobs at all. They were never in love with the idea of an IT career in the first place; they were merely in love with everything they thought they would get with an IT career—like an instant job, the chance to wear shorts and flip-flops to work, and the ability to cash in their stock options and retire at 33.

Labor market forecasts are just that: forecasts. Moreover, they represent only one factor to consider in your career decision making. Other essential variables—like your skills and abilities, your interests, and your values—are not only much more predictable, they are also more reliable indicators of the academic major and career you should ultimately pursue.

Today's "hot" can too easily become tomorrow's "not." And the next "sure thing" may turn out to be pure sting. So treat labor market forecasts like the fragile packages they are: handle with care.

Highlight This: Labor market forecasts are predictions, not facts. It is fine to take them under advisement in your career decision making; just do not give them full power over your ultimate choices.

Money, Status, and Power Are Not the Only Forms of Pay

Values are the emotional salary of work, and some folks are drawing no wages at all.

Howard Figler

By 1994, Russ Blanck had been an attorney for 12 years. He was at a point in his career where he was pulling down a comfortable six-figure income and he had earned the prestige that goes along with any successful career in law. But something was bugging him: He could not quite put his finger on it, but he was vaguely dissatisfied with his work. Why? "Because there was no social utility to what I was doing anymore," says Blanck, now 48. "I wasn't making anyone or anything better from a global perspective." Even though he was being paid handsomely when it came to his finances and his reputation, he wasn't making enough of what he had come to value most: a social contribution.

It was then that he made a decision that ultimately changed his career—and his life—though neither was his intent at the time: At age 36, Blanck enrolled at the police academy. He had no plans of actually becoming a police officer; he simply wanted to gain both the experience and the respect necessary to continue working with the law enforcement clients he had lately come to be helping in his legal role.

But as Blanck happily shares today, a funny thing happened on his way to becoming a lawyer with a law enforcement background; he instead decided to become a law enforcement professional with a law background. When he finished his two-year police training in 1996, he took a part-time police officer position—on top of his full-time attorney job—with the Centennial Lakes Police Department in suburban Minneapolis/St. Paul. Two years after that he left his career as an attorney to become a cop full time with the department, a job he loves to this day—despite the fact that it pays less than half what his old job did.

Our American culture is pretty clear on what it values most. Typically money, status, and power are where it is at—and it is money, status, and power that will ultimately make a person happy in his or her career, the logic goes. That is what Russ Blanck was led to believe, in great part due to the influence of his parents, who gave him two career options to choose from after he graduated from high school in 1975: law or medicine. He chose law, he says, because "I wasn't good with blood." Only much later did he begin to understand that there were other forms of "pay" to consider where one's career is concerned.

What do you want most in your working life? What if you are driven primarily by something other than money, status, and power? It is a critical question for you to think about, especially now as you consider the career path you will pursue after college. It is not an easy thing to do when you are a twentysomething, Blanck acknowledges. "But you have to somehow find the curiosity to investigate what you will be in five years, ten years, fifteen years," he says. "Whatever that is has to have some meaning to you—and, in a perfect world, to people outside of you as well."

Blanck's experience—and the wisdom that has resulted from it—illustrates a troubling but common truth: We tend not to identify (or even think about) what is really important to us in our work until years after our college days are behind us. Only when we find ourselves "lost in the wilderness"—perhaps in our late twenties or our thirties or even beyond—do we begin to assess what we really want from our careers and figure out how to make positive changes in our work lives.

While being "lost" is useful sometimes, it is not much fun. You can avoid the associated feelings of frustration and despair if you take some time now to really figure out what you want most in your future career. Perhaps earning a high income, being in a prestigious career, and having a great deal of authority really are your most cherished work-related values. That is just fine, and you can use that knowledge to find a career offering those benefits. On the other hand, maybe you are driven more by something else, something like:

Your Need for Independence. Do you get frustrated by bureaucracy? Do you thrive on being your own boss and making your own decisions? If so, *independence* ought to be a key variable you look for in your future career. Maybe, in the grand scheme of things, you are willing to compromise on or even forgo money, status, and power for the chance to call most or even all of your own shots.

Your Need for Creativity. Do you enjoy building something from nothing? Do you cringe when someone you are working with says, "We have always done it this way"? If so, *creative expression* ought to be something you look for in your future career. Perhaps you are willing to compromise on or even forgo money, status, and power for the sake of developing and implementing your own innovative ideas.

Your Need to Make a Difference. Do you want to do work that helps other people? Are there local or global "wrongs" that you would like to address? If so, *altruism* and *contribution* are certainly traits you will need to look for in your future career. You are probably willing to compromise on or forgo money, status, and power for the opportunity to contribute something beneficial to society—to do something that really matters and that will leave a lasting legacy.

Your Need to Have a Life Away from Work. Do you wince when you hear of people working 60 or 70 hours a week? Would you like to have clear boundaries between your job and your home life? If so, *balance* is a key component you should look for in your future career. You are no doubt willing to compromise on or forgo money, status, and power so that your work stays at work and does not interfere with your family, your hobbies, and your play.

There are dozens of other work-related values for you to consider, of course, and it is a process that takes time and effort, not to mention a bit of soul searching. So you may want to get some help with it, perhaps from a career counselor at your school. Most every college or university in the country has a career center or similar office staffed by well-trained professionals who can help you with this important task. Just remember that as you go through the values identification process, you are trying to determine *your* most-cherished work values—not those of your family, your friends, your professors, or other people in your life. Ultimately, only you will live out the career decisions you make, whatever they may be.

"So try and listen to your heart," Blanck stresses. "Try to figure out what sends *you*."

Highlight This: Your career belongs to *you*—not your parents, your siblings, your friends, your professors, or anyone else. You are the one who will have to live each day with the career choices you make (or fail to make). Choose what is best for *you*.

It Is Hard to Make Career Decisions When You Are Dealing with Other Serious Issues

What does not destroy me makes me strong.

Friedrich Nietzsche

It is difficult enough to make important career decisions when your mind is clear and your physical, emotional, and psychological health are fairly solid. But if you are dealing with other life-impacting situations too, it can be nearly impossible—not to mention unwise—to move ahead.

When I was in graduate school at the University of Wisconsin-Whitewater, my fellow graduate assistant in the career center, Kathy Craney, was in a session with a client and sensed something was very, very wrong with the young woman—something that went far beyond what major she should pick. "Are you suicidal?" Kathy came right out and asked. "Yes," the young woman replied. And with that, the two of them walked together to the campus health center, where the student could get the anything-but-career-related help she really needed at the time.

Your career exploration and decision-making activities do not happen in a vacuum. Indeed, while you are trying to figure out what career might fit you best, you might also be struggling with one or more of an assortment of debilitating issues. Do any of the following scenarios sound like you? If so, you may need to set your career concerns aside for a while and focus on more pressing issues instead:

Depression. Clinical depression has been called the common cold of mental health, and for good reason: The National Institute of Mental Health notes that in any given one-year period, 18.8 million American adults suffer from a depressive illness. The numbers are even more troubling on college campuses. The National Mental Health Association estimates that more than 10 percent of American college students have been diagnosed with depression, and the American College Health Association found in 2004 that 14.9 percent of surveyed students had been diagnosed with depression.

Is it possible you are going through depression right now? Are you sleeping much more or much less than usual? Are you losing interest in people and activities that normally make you happy? Are you cranky and exhausted? All of these signs are potential symptoms of clinical depression. Visit your school's counseling center or health service to learn more—and to get help if you need it.

Anxiety. One of depression's close cousins (because the two often go hand in hand), anxiety can wreak havoc in your life. If you are on edge—nervous, tense, bouncing off the walls—and you feel like you are not getting everything done or that something bad is going to happen to you if you do (or do not do) a particular something, you might well be suffering from an anxiety disorder. Again, visit your school's counseling center or health service to be assessed.

Trauma. Perhaps your family just lost their home to a fire. Maybe you were abused by someone as a child or you recently were assaulted by someone you thought you could trust. We all face problems every day, but some—like these and many others—rise to the level of being traumas. If you have suffered some kind of trauma, your career concerns should fall to about number 10 on your list of priorities. Head for your school's counseling center or health service and ask for help.

Money (or Lack Thereof). How can you possibly worry about the major you are going to select or the career you are going to get into when you are afraid you are not going to be able to pay for the privilege of pursuing either one of them? The college students of today are, as a group, having a difficult time coping with the escalating costs of a college education. The frequent results: overwhelming student loan and credit card debt, for starters, and even bankruptcy in some cases. A visit to your school's financial-aid office is in order if money is running your academic life right now. (You could also see if your family works with a financial planner who might be of some help to you where money is concerned.)

Grades. Maybe you are on the verge of flunking out of school—or, a bit less seriously, you are failing one of your classes or you just bombed the chemistry midterm. Frustration and concern are the natural fallout you will be dealing with—fallout that will definitely inhibit your career decision-making activities. Talk to your academic advisor to see what your school offers in the way of tutoring and academic counseling services. Once you get your grades back up, you will be in a better mood to get on with career-related activities.

Substance Abuse. Often, substance abuse is not easily recognized by the person you see in the mirror each day. Usually, the people around you—close friends and family, especially—start asking you whether you have a problem with alcohol and/or other drugs. Do you? Are you sure? Your career concerns can wait; take care of your substance abuse issues first. A campus counselor or physician can help you get started.

Relationship Problems. Perhaps you left your significant other back home—700 miles away—to attend college, and things between the two of you are now strained on even the best days. Or maybe your father is pressing you to your breaking point to become an accounting major when you have absolutely no interest in that particular path. The people in our lives have an enormous impact on not only our happiness, but also our level-headedness. If one or more of your important personal relationships is in shambles, your career issues need to take a backseat temporarily. Work with a campus counselor to dissect the stressful relationship(s) and learn how to make it healthy again—or even end it if necessary.

The major you choose and the career you end up going into are important. But your psyche is more important, for it drives—among many other things—your career exploration and decision-making activities. So if your psyche is in trouble right now, for whatever reason, first things first: Deal with your psyche. Get yourself back into physical, psychological, and emotional shape. Then you can get back to your career concerns with an uncluttered mind.

Highlight This: If you are not thinking clearly, your career decisions can wait. Focus on your overall psychological health first.

Confront Your Conclusions

You Are Not the Only One Who Is Struggling to Decide

You may say I'm a dreamer, but I'm not the only one.

John Lennon

I love being alone sometimes. But I cannot stand being lonely—and that is how I often felt during my college years when I was trying to figure out what major to choose and what career path to pursue after graduation.

Loneliness is bad enough when you are alone. But it is even worse when you look around and see that everyone else in your life is anything but lonely. That, too, is how I felt during college; my friends had everything figured out (or so it seemed), while I was the loser who could not figure anything out. My overriding daily thought was, "Why am *I* so lost when everyone else is so focused and sure?"

If you are feeling that way right now, I have news for you: You are not alone. You are not even remotely close to being alone, for much of the "decisiveness" you see surrounding you is an illusion.

That roommate of yours who has known she has wanted to be a doctor since the fifth grade? Not so fast. It is quite possible that she is being pushed in that direction by her parents. Instead of resisting, she is not only going along with the idea, she is also putting on one heck of a front to convince herself and others that it is her own career goal. Why? Because it is easier to deal with something you do not want if you can convince yourself you really do want it.

That friend of yours who is an accounting major? You have no clue how or why he chose that path. It could well be that he simply picked it for its future job prospects (at least as he perceives them). He might also have become an accounting major because it was the first degree he saw on the alphabetical list of majors on your school's Web site—and anything, he figured, was better than being constantly referred to as "undecided" or "undeclared."

Just how many college students like you are truly undecided about their major or future career (whether they want to admit it or not)? Let's look at the evidence:

- In the 2006 *Graduating Student & Alumni* survey conducted by the National Association of Colleges and Employers (NACE) (a professional association made up of college and university career services professionals and employers who hire college students for internships and entry-level positions), 16.1 percent of the 7,015 college students surveyed admitted they had "sort of drifted" into the majors they ultimately chose. (Important note: The students across the United States who participate in this annual survey are the ones who are motivated enough to go to their campus career centers and pick up a copy of NACE's annual *Job Choices* magazine, in which the survey instrument appears. It is almost certain that the 16.1 percent figure is significantly higher, since the majority of less-motivated students are not apt to visit their school's career center, let alone pick up a magazine and fill out a survey once there.)

- In the 2006 *Toolbox Revisited* study conducted by the U.S. Department of Education's National Center for Education Statistics, half of the college students who were tracked over the course of eight years reported changing their major at least once during college. Are you enrolled at a relatively small school of, say, 2,000 students? Nine hundred ninety-nine of them besides you are wavering at least a little about the major and career they should pursue. Most of them may hide it well; but that does not mean they are not struggling on the inside.

When you do not have as much life experience as, say, a 40-year-old, and you have dozens of majors and hundreds of careers to choose from, and you are busy enough just trying to keep up with your classes and your job(s) and your relationship(s), is it any wonder you are not quite sure what academic path and future career you want to pursue? And similarly, is it any wonder that many of your fellow students are wrestling with the very same problems, whether they acknowledge it publicly or not?

You probably hate going to a restaurant where the waiter hands you a complicated 10-page menu—possibly written in another language—and then stands there tapping his foot with a sneer on his face as he pushes you to make an immediate decision on what to order. How do you invariably respond? One of two ways:

- You pick something hurriedly just to shut the waiter up—a "decision" of sorts—and you then end up regretting your choice once it is placed in front of you.

- You ask the waiter to come back in a few minutes so that you can take the time you need to study your options and make a wise decision.

When it comes to choosing majors and careers, some of your fellow college students have selected the shut-the-waiter-up option for now. Others—like you, perhaps—have opted for the come-back-in-a-few-minutes path. The result in each case: a whole lot of students who are still trying to figure out what academic and career paths are best for them.

Ironically, they think they are all alone too. But they are not—and neither are you.

Highlight This: You are not the only one who is struggling with the tasks of choosing a major and a future career path. You are just one of the relatively few college students who is willing to admit it.

Eliminate an Option Only If You Have Thoroughly Investigated It

Most ignorance is vincible ignorance:
We don't know because we don't want to know.

Aldous Huxley

Every interest assessment I have ever taken has suggested that I might match up well with a career in counseling. Yet until comparatively recently, I dismissed the possibility out of hand, with a snicker and a "yeah, right."

If you have ever taken an interest assessment, you have undoubtedly done the same thing. Perhaps you were looking at your results when your roommate saw what you were doing and asked what the test came up with. "It says I should be a tax accountant," you replied—before both you and your roommate began howling with laughter. "Or listen to this," you added, "a perfusionist."

"What the hell is that?" came your roommate's incredulous reply. You could not respond because you did not know either—you figured it had something to do with perfume. So perfusionist immediately fell off your career radar screen, and tax accountant quickly followed. Elapsed time: again, probably 10 seconds or so. You eliminated from consideration not one but two careers, in less time than it takes you to brush your teeth. You have probably given more thought to deciding what shirt to wear in the morning.

And yet you were the one who responded to a hundred or more questions on the interest assessment. Assuming you answered accurately and honestly, there is no reason to believe the test developers are lying to you or playing a joke on you. They have spent many years and many more dollars creating these instruments, after all, and it is safe to believe they have done their best to ensure their assessments provide reliable, valid information.

So what is going on? It's simple: The human mind, in an effort to manage ever-increasing amounts of information, tends to take shortcuts whenever possible, using tools like beliefs, assumptions, and perceptions to make quick judgments and even quicker decisions. It is just faster to, for example, blow off a career as a perfusionist than to actually investigate the field thoroughly. When you do that, though, you take a low-level but nonetheless real risk: You just might end up blowing off a career that would have brought you years or even a lifetime of satisfaction.

When I look back, I really have no idea why I never took the counseling idea seriously. In many ways it is a puzzling contradiction. I am one to frequently ponder matters of psychological functioning, for example, most often by myself on the front stoop of my house, but on occasion with my wife and others in my life as well. I have pretty good listening skills, I can put together a presentation (à la a seminar or a class) that is entertaining and thought-provoking at the same time, I am friendly and (mostly) nonjudgmental, and I genuinely enjoy helping people. It is no wonder the interest assessments always included counseling in their lists of careers I ought to explore. And yet my explorations of the field were never more than glimpses—if that, even. Had it not been for my first postgraduation job in publishing—one that gave me the chance to interview college counselors for articles—I might have, quite literally, missed my calling in life. Conversely, if I had considered my interest assessment results a bit more carefully, I might have heard that calling sooner. It is much easier to hear, after all, when you are actually listening!

I encourage you not to make this same mistake. Whether you are considering various careers or exploring different majors, make yourself the following promise: "I will eliminate a reasonable option only if I have thoroughly investigated it." The key word here is "reasonable." You cannot thoroughly explore the more than 20,000 occupations that exist in the world of work; it just is not possible. But you can go beyond a cursory glance once you have narrowed down your options using tools like interest assessments or career counseling. When you do, pay special attention to:

Careers You Have Never Heard Of. Do you know what a *perfusionist* is? Most people don't. No perfume here. A perfusionist is someone who operates the heart-lung machine that keeps a patient alive during surgery. Suppose you are interested in health-care careers, broadly speaking. How would you feel years after the fact if you had dismissed the results of an interest assessment suggesting you might enjoy a career as a perfusionist—when you have finally learned what it is? What if you realized it could have been a great career match for you? You would be kicking yourself big-time.

Careers You Have Heard of and Potentially Misjudged. We have all heard of lawyers, but most of us have little idea of what they really do each day and all the various settings where they work. A lawyer is not a lawyer is not a lawyer. Just ask an intellectual property attorney to compare her job with that of a defense attorney—and ask the two of them to compare their jobs with that of a public-interest attorney for a nonprofit agency. There is what you *know* about a particular career and there is what you *think you know*; usually, there is a canyon of difference between the two.

It is bad enough to go down a career path that does not really fit you. But it is nothing short of tragic to miss—or ignore—road signs that have been trying to point you in the right direction all along. You will not spot them if you are not watching for them.

Highlight This: The career option you know little or nothing about today might be the very career you will find satisfying tomorrow—but only if you take the time to investigate it.

PART III

BUILD YOUR SKILLS AND EXPERIENCE THROUGH HANDS-ON ACTIVITIES

Introduction

Experience Leads to Skills; Skills Lead to Jobs

Experience is a good school, but the fees are high.

Heinrich Heine

Two college students, both about to enter their senior year, are competing for the same summer internship in a midsize public relations firm. One of the students is a public relations major. The other is majoring in sociology. Who gets the position?

If your answer is "the PR major," you are wrong. If your answer is "the sociology major," you are still wrong! The correct answer is counterintuitive. The student who gets the internship is the one who has the best *skills* in the eyes of the people making the hiring decision—no matter what that student is majoring in.

As a college student, you naturally and understandably spend most if not all of your academic career worrying about choosing and completing the "right" major. But you know what you are going to discover when you head for the real world after graduation? Practically speaking, employers do not give a damn about what you majored in; they give a damn about what you can do as a result of the experiences you gained—in and out of the classroom, in a variety of settings and situations—during your college years.

Some of those experiences, of course, will indeed come from the courses you take in your particular major. Employers know that. There is a reason, for instance, that most employers hiring entry-level accountants want applicants to be accounting or perhaps finance majors: they are looking for reasonable evidence that the candidates will have the ground-level, core knowledge necessary to handle the basics of the job. The coursework in any accounting or finance major practically guarantees that much. But that is as far as the criterion goes—for employers also know that the fact one is an accounting or finance major says absolutely nothing about whether he or she ultimately has the skills necessary to do the job well.

Thus, the right sociology major can easily outmaneuver a public relations major for a public relations internship. Suppose the sociology major has already done an internship as a staff member for a state legislator. Maybe that internship required the sociology major to handle correspondence with the legislator's constituents, write and distribute news releases covering the legislator's activities, and set up the legislator's various town meetings in cities around the district. Perhaps the sociology major writes a weekly column for the campus newspaper as well.

Suppose the public relations major, on the other hand, has no previous PR-related experience. She has never even held a part-time job. She has spent her entire high school and now college existence focusing completely on her courses—no working, no interning, no volunteering, no participating in campus activities, no pursuits beyond the classroom. All she has so far are the skills she has developed through her academic activities. On its face, there is nothing wrong with that; she is competing for an internship, after all, not a management job. But if you are an employer looking for a PR intern and you are comparing this particular PR major with this particular sociology major, who really appears to be the better candidate? At best, the contest is too close to call—though plenty of employers would immediately point to the sociology major as the wiser choice for the position. Her major has been rendered irrelevant; her skills have carried the day.

If you have the skills employers are looking for, your major will not matter as much as it otherwise might. It may not even matter at all. The reverse, however, is also true: The "right" major is not worth much if you do not have the skills to back it up. Employers do not hire majors; they hire skills and abilities. And the most valuable skills and abilities—the ones that matter most in the world of work—tend to emerge from your experiences, whether they are paid or unpaid. Experiences lead to skills. Skills in turn lead to the jobs and other opportunities that, put together, become your successful career.

Focus on Action

At Some Point, You Have to Stop Planning and Start Doing

To launch ourselves anew, we need to get out of our heads. We need to act.

Herminia Ibarra

Got a question for you—and I swear it is not a trick question. Suppose your car is stuck in the mud. In this scenario, what does "stuck" mean?

"Well, Sherlock," you might reply, "it just means you're ... you know, stuck."

Not quite. Think harder.

"You're stuck. You can't get going. You're not *moving!*"

Bingo! "You're not *moving.*" That is the answer I was looking for.

"I'm stuck" is one of the most common ways college students describe themselves to career counselors like me. Early in my career, I became as frustrated as my clients when I heard them say "I'm stuck." But over the last few years—thanks in particular to the work of four career professionals who wrote three off-the-beaten path career success books—I have learned that there is a simple solution to the "I'm stuck" problem: You need to get *moving.*

I mean that in the most literal way; if you are feeling stuck in your career decision making as a college student, you need to take some action—any action will do, at least at first—to begin getting (and feeling) "unstuck." At some point in your college career—hopefully sooner than later—you need to stop planning and thinking and analyzing and start *doing* instead, even though you do not know where your actions will ultimately lead.

Kathleen Mitchell, author of the insightful book *The Unplanned Career: How to Turn Curiosity into Opportunity* (Chronicle Books, 2003), has an oxymoronic name for this act-and-learn method of career exploration and decision making: *planned happenstance.* Many of her career counseling clients at City College of San Francisco have described the approach in a single powerful word: liberating.

"This idea that you need to spend time figuring out exactly what you want before taking action—in my experience, that's exactly what blocks people," says Mitchell. "If you don't want a career, spend time planning it. If, on the other hand, you want a career, then just take some action and be ready for unplanned events you'll cause as a result of your action."

Here is a quick experiment for you: Next time you are home for a break from college, ask your parents and a few other adults in your life how they came to work in the jobs or careers they are in right now. You will almost certainly discover that the majority of the people you talk to have followed paths that have been winding, not straight—roads riddled with potholes and dead ends, not smooth, easy-to-follow freeways with brand-new asphalt.

Even we career counselors—the people in this world who preach something called *career planning*—tend not to have planned our own careers. For more than five years now, I have been conducting an informal, one-question poll among my career-counseling colleagues: "When you were in high school or college, did you plan to become a career counselor someday?" So far, not a single career counselor has said yes. In terms of baseball batting statistics, we career counselors are 0-for-everything when it comes to planning our own careers. Along the way we have learned some things—sometimes for better, other times for worse—and stumbled upon opportunities that we either have taken advantage of or regret *not* having taken advantage of.

Welcome to career development in the 21st century.

Yes, you should do the best you can to analyze yourself and the world of work, starting as early in your college career as possible. (I have been harping about just that, after all, in the first half of this very book!) But you do not—and cannot—learn by thinking alone, and you certainly do not—and cannot—make informed career decisions that way. You also have to *do*; you have to *act*—and then *react* (and re-act) as circumstances unfold and opportunities present themselves along the way.

The way you act can be as simple as volunteering somewhere for a week or talking to someone about her career. Or you can go a step or two further by getting a part-time job or an internship in a field you think you might enjoy. Herminia Ibarra, author of the book *Working Identity: Unconventional Strategies for Reinventing Your Career* (Harvard Business School Press, 2003), calls this process *crafting experiments*, which "refers to the practice of implementing the small probes and projects that allow us to try out new professional roles on a limited but tangible scale without committing to a particular direction."

The beauty of such an action-oriented process is that it does not require a mind-set of permanence, stresses Stanford University psychologist John Krumboltz, coauthor (with Al Levin) of the book *Luck Is No Accident: Making the Most of Happenstance in Your Life and Career* (Impact Publishers, 2004). "We take the point of view," he says, "that it's better to speak of what would be fun to try next rather than what you're going to do for the rest of your life."

No matter what happens as a result of the actions you begin taking, you can't lose. If you learn, for instance, that you really do like a particular career or industry, great! If, on the other hand, you discover that a particular field is not for you, wonderful! Now you will not waste any more time, energy, and money on it in college—to say nothing of the years or even decades after college.

Whether your actions help you determine a career path that fits or a career path that does not, the return on investment is the same: You will not only emerge from the mud; you will also get back on the road—*moving* toward a career destination.

Highlight This: Career planning is wasted effort if it never turns into career action. At some point, you need to stop planning and start *doing*—even if you do not know exactly what the results will be.

Experience Is Not Optional; It Is Essential

In the business world, everyone is paid in two coins: cash and experience. Take the experience first; the cash will come later.

Harold Geneen

If I had to identify the top three most universally frustrating career issues among college students, the notion of *experience* (or, more accurately, lack thereof) would surely be one of them. Indeed, one of the most frequent job-related questions I get from college students and recent graduates—whether I am meeting them in person or "talking" to them via MonsterTRAK's Career Planning for College Students message board—goes something like this: Why do employers expect you to have experience when you need to have a job in the first place in order to *get* experience?

It is a fair question. But in the mind of an employer—someone who ultimately has to pay you (or whoever is hired) a good little chunk of the organization's hard-earned money—it is also an irrelevant question. To the typical entry-level employers of today, experience is no longer the optional add-on it once was where candidates are concerned; to employers, experience is essential—and something they can and do demand of students and recent grads, whether you like it or not. Why? There are several reasons, all of which you can easily understand (though you still may not agree with them) if you put yourself in the hiring manager's shoes:

Too Many Students and Grads Do Have Experience. We have reached a point now when most college students graduate with experience of some kind, whether it is through an internship, a co-op, a job, or some other activity (see **Internship Is Just One Name for Valuable Experience**, p. 140). Thus, if you are one of the relatively few college students who approaches employers with no experience of any kind, you just cannot compete with most of your peers—and the employers know it. Remember: The test known as your job search is graded on a curve (see **This Test Is Graded on a Curve**, p. 199); employers will evaluate you not in *isolation from* other students or grads, but in *comparison to* other students or grads.

Students Who Have Experience Are Perceived as More Focused and Skilled. There may be very good reasons why you have no experience in your chosen field yet. Perhaps you double- or triple-majored and simply did not have the time (or the money) to do much more. Perhaps you were taking care of your family the whole time you were in school. Maybe you yourself were sick for a time during college and it was all you could do to get back on your feet and graduate. All well and good.

But employers tend to read the worst into your lack of experience. For starters, they will question your dedication to the field you are trying to get into. "If this student didn't do an internship," a public relations hiring manager might think to herself, "then how do I know he's really into PR as a career? How can I be sure he is not dabbling and that he won't quit on me three months from now?" More importantly, employers tend to question the skills and abilities of students who have no experience in their chosen field. To an employer, it is one thing to be able to write a paper or work on a team as part of a class, but it is quite another to be able to do the same things—and do them well—in a professional work setting where the stakes are much higher.

Students with Experience Are Seen as Needing Less Training. The more time and money an employer has to invest in training you (or whoever is hired) in the tasks of the job—not to mention the nuances of the organization and the quirks of the people there—the more it costs to hire you. Thus, if you are a human resources management (HRM) major and you interned last summer in the training and development department of a *Fortune* 500 company—where, among other things, you developed PowerPoint presentations—you already know PowerPoint well enough to be a legitimate asset. For all a prospective employer knows, the other student who is competing with you for the job only fiddled around with PowerPoint for five minutes in a class one time—if she fiddled with it at all. Thus, hiring your competitor will cost the employer at least a $395 "Basics of PowerPoint" course, not to mention a day or two of missed work for that new hire as she learns the software. Bringing you on board, conversely, will be as simple as showing you your computer, saying "there's PowerPoint," and telling you to get started.

In the eyes of employers, then, the more experience you have, the more you will stand out compared to your peers who are not experienced. Employers will see you as more focused and dedicated to your chosen field, and the less handholding you will need once you are on the job, the better. It all adds up, fairly or unfairly, to an entry-level employment environment where experience is required—and lack of experience will prevent you from being hired.

Highlight This: The days when you can graduate from college without experience are long gone. Get as much experience as you can during college, no matter what you need to do to pull it off. Experience is no longer optional; it is essential.

Internship Is Just One Name for Valuable Experience

It is equally a mistake to hold oneself too high or to rate oneself too cheap.

Johann von Goethe

The term *internship* gets thrown around so much—by college students, college parents, and college and university staff—that you might think an internship is the only way to obtain valuable experience while you are in school, and that internship experience is somehow the only type of experience that will be taken seriously by future employers. Indeed, you may go even further and mistakenly believe that until you have done an internship—and that the experience is actually *called* an internship—you have done nothing at all as far as prospective employers are concerned.

Internship, internship, internship!

My eyes were opened to this troubling phenomenon by Brian (not his real name), who showed up in my office at the University of Wisconsin-Whitewater career center one day and told me—and I quote: "I really haven't done anything." It was his way of saying he had not participated in an internship, and that he was about to graduate with nothing that could possibly be of interest to prospective employers.

So I asked him what he had done during his college years. Turns out he had worked—full time—at a nearby restaurant for the previous three years. But that was just the beginning of the eye-opening tale that unfolded over the next hour or so. In that time, I also learned that Brian:

- Had been promoted to assistant manager of the restaurant before he had even finished working there for a year, and that he had since been promoted to manager—a position he had held for about two years by the time he came to see me.

- Had hired and trained more than 20 employees of the restaurant, starting when he was assistant manager and continuing when he became manager.

- Was bilingual in English and Spanish, and that he had used his Spanish fluency to oversee the training of all new employees whose first language was Spanish.

- Was solely responsible for not only adding up the restaurant's sales totals each day, but also bringing the cash and checks to the bank and depositing the money in the after-hours deposit box.

In his own mind, though, Brian had not "done anything" during the previous three years—in part because his experience was not called an internship and in part because he wanted to go into education (not the restaurant business) as a profession.

Then Brian's story continued. He went on to tell me that in the little spare time he had, he volunteered at a technical college some 25 miles away. His role there was using his Spanish background to help out in English as a second language (ESL) courses for recent immigrants. At first Brian merely served as an assistant to another ESL instructor. Before long, though, the instructor saw Brian's skill—not to mention his potential—and recommended that he become a full-fledged course co-instructor, which he did.

But he had not "done anything" in that role either—because (you guessed it) the experience was not called an internship.

It took the rest of that 50-minute session and most of another for me to convince Brian that what his diverse and impressive experiences were called would not make much difference to future employers. That he had the experiences is what mattered.

The same is true for you. *Internship* is just one name for the valuable experience you can gain during your college years. Here are a few other names for it that will grab the attention of future employers:

A Co-op Experience. A *co-op* is quite similar to an internship, but it is even more extensive in most cases. Typically when you are a co-op student, you alternate between attending school full time one semester and working (in your co-op) full time the next. Essentially, a co-op is a job—specifically, a job that closely relates to the field or industry you are interested in pursuing after graduation.

A Job. Brian's restaurant gig was not an internship or a co-op; it was a plain old *job*, and it was an outstanding one at that. Perhaps you have worked for two summers at a camp back in your hometown, and you will be heading back there again this summer to be assistant camp director. Nobody there has ever referred to you as an intern. Who cares? The skills you are learning and the traits you are developing each day will still be of interest to prospective employers, whether you are called *employee* or *intern* or *assistant camp king* or *queen*!

A Volunteer Experience. Nobody called you an intern when you helped build a house for Habitat for Humanity. Nor did anyone call you an intern when you volunteered in the surgery waiting room at a nearby hospital last semester, keeping worried people posted about their loved ones' progress on the operating table. It does not matter; the work you did—out of the goodness of your heart—gave you experiences you can market to prospective employers.

An Externship (Job Shadow). Perhaps you "shadowed" an alum from your school last month as she went about her everyday tasks as a certified public accountant. You spent only a couple of days with her—nothing earth-shattering—but while you were there you were able to confirm your choice to become a CPA after graduation. And your shadowee also had you do some minor administrative tasks during your time together, which gave you the chance to polish your Microsoft Excel skills. Your externship may not be *the* experience you market to future employers, but it is definitely *one* experience you can market to future employers.

A Study/Work Abroad Experience. Just before you boarded the plane for Spain last May to spend the summer studying at Universitat de Barcelona, you panicked as you wondered whether you would be able to handle being away from home for three months and, especially, be able to adjust to a brand new culture. When you arrived, you were indeed anxious for a day or two. Then you discovered that you could not only survive but also thrive in another country. You even managed to land a tutoring job that kept you essentially debt-free while you were across the pond. Nope, it wasn't an internship; but it *was* an experience to sell to a would-be employer.

A Student Leadership Experience. You are the unpaid but dedicated sports editor of your school's student newspaper. The articles you are writing, the visibility you are getting, and the contacts you are making will more than compensate for the fact that no one is running around calling you *intern*.

What's in a name? Not much when it comes to obtaining useful experience during your college years. Do not get stuck on the concept of internship. If you are going to get stuck on anything, get stuck on the concept of *experience*—in any or all of its many forms.

Highlight This: Experience does not have to be called an *internship* to be valuable in the eyes of potential employers.

Internships and Co-ops Give You a Competitive Advantage

By far the best proof is experience.

Sir Francis Bacon

I will never forget my first internship. It was in the sports department of the *Forum*, a daily newspaper in Fargo, North Dakota, just across the Red River from Minnesota and my school, Moorhead State University, where I was majoring in mass communications. By day, I would attend my classes and learn, among other things, what a career in journalism *would be* like. By night, I learned what a career in journalism *was* like.

In my classes, I would usually have at least several days—often longer—to come up with an article or a paper. At the *Forum*, it was not unusual to have *minutes* to write a piece that someone would be reading (or so I hoped) over breakfast less than 12 hours later. Sure, many of the pieces were just a paragraph or two. But when I covered a basketball game that ran until 9:30 p.m. and I didn't get back to the office until 10:10 and I had to produce 14 inches of copy by 10:30 or else (failure was not an option), I learned not only how to write well but also how to write fast, and with the eyes of an equally stressed layout editor glaring at me. I also learned how to write 14 inches of copy. Not 13 and certainly not 15 or 16. Fourteen. If the layout editor had saved a 14-inch "hole" for my story, then my article had to be 14 inches long. To paraphrase Johnny Cochran: "If it doesn't fit, you must edit."

In my classes, I would do group projects with a close and trusted friend (or two or three); I could almost always choose whom I wanted to work with, and if necessary I could do most of the work myself if I really wanted to. But at the *Forum*, I had no choice as to whom I would be working with on a given night. I had to do a good job with whoever I was paired up with. While everyone I worked with was great and ultimately helped me immensely in my career, I reacted very differently to different people, especially where the layout editors were concerned.

Mark, for example, was only a few years older than I was and was in my mass communications program at Moorhead State. He had worked his way up to a layout editing position after starting at the *Forum* at the ripe old age of 15. Mark was always the epitome of calm, at least on the outside, and I could tell that while he expected solid work from me and everyone else, he would handle any problems he had with me quietly and behind the scenes. Steve, on the other hand, was a different story. Steve reminded me of "The Crusher" from All-Star Wrestling, and he was intense. Nice—especially once you got to know him a little better—but intense nonetheless. I was basically afraid of Steve, which perhaps explains why I never made a major mistake in his presence; I was worried he would kick my butt, literally and figuratively, right then and there in front of the entire night newsroom staff. So while I never would have chosen to work with Steve, I had to learn how to do it and do it well.

In my classes, we would always get detailed feedback on our performance, from peers and instructors alike. We were graded on most everything, obviously, but we would also receive commentary, both in writing and in person, that we could then use to improve our writing. At the *Forum*, there just was not time for feedback. If you were to turn in a piece and then sit around waiting for sentence-by-sentence analysis from the layout editor or another staffer, you would be waiting indefinitely. Sure, you would get the occasional "nice job on that one" or "good story," but that would immediately be followed up with a look that said, "Get back to work."

I did not understand back then what is so crystal clear to me now where internships and their *co-op* cousins (see **Internship Is Just One Name for Valuable Experience**, p. 140) are concerned: Internships and co-ops serve as the real-world portion of your college education that you simply cannot, do not, and will not get in your classes. That is why internship and co-op experience puts you at an undisputed competitive advantage in the eyes of the employers who will one day consider you for a job after graduation.

Why does a new grad with internship or co-op experience look so much better to the typical employer than a new grad without such experience? Because employers tend to make several positive assumptions about students who have completed internships and/or co-ops:

They Are Committed To Their Chosen Fields. Suppose you are a hiring manager and you notice on a student's résumé that he has done a couple of co-ops as well as a summer internship. Two of those experiences are directly related to the work your organization does, and the third is a sensible complement to the others. What do you read into this student's candidacy? Among other things, you can pretty safely assume that the student is in your field for the long haul. If he were merely dabbling or undecided about his future, he would not have bothered to do more than one internship or co-op in the same general discipline.

As important, if you hire this particular student, he or she will be much more likely to stay with your organization than will a student who lacks internship or co-op experience. In a 2005 survey of employers conducted by the National Association of Colleges and Employers, nearly 80 percent of the respondents reported higher retention rates among college hires who had internship and/or co-op experience versus those who did not.

They Have Developed the Essential Skills and Traits They Will Need to Succeed. For starters, students with internship or co-op experience will almost certainly have the *hard skills* or *technical skills* they will need on the job. A computer science major, for instance, will know how to write real, functioning software programs. A journalism student like I was will have proven skill in writing articles to fit 14-inch holes in 20 minutes or less! As important, though, intern and co-op students develop the crucial *soft skills* every 21st-century worker needs: written and verbal communication skills, the ability to work well in groups, leadership abilities, research skills, and analytical skills, among many others.

They Have References Who Can Be Specific Versus General. When it comes to the value of your professional references, there is "no comparison" between your internship or co-op supervisor and, for example, one of your professors, says Terese Corey Blanck, director of student development for Roseville, Minnesota-based Student Experience (http://www.studentexperience.com), a company that offers personal care assistant (PCA) internships to Twin Cities college students who want to gain skills in helping people with disabilities.

"A professor can tell me how a student does academically but not how that student does in the workplace," says Corey Blanck, who has screened, interviewed, and hired thousands of college students in her 20-plus-year career in both higher education and the private sector. "Students who have internship or co-op experience have at least one reference I can call to get *specific* answers to *specific* questions I have about their strengths, their work ethic, and their commitment to their chosen field. That's what really helps me make a sound decision about whether to hire a student or not."

They Understand the Real World of Work, with All of Its Stresses, Uncertainties, and Quirks. A new accounting graduate who has completed an internship with a public accounting firm will not be shocked when her 40-hour week turns into a 60- or

70-hour week during tax season; she will have seen it—or even experienced it to a degree—during her internship. A student whose six-month co-op was a lesson in office politics more than anything else will have no trouble adjusting to a company where major decisions sometimes ride not on sound analysis of the facts but on who the boss's favorites are.

My internship at the *Forum* was exciting and exhausting, helpful and stressful—all at the same time. Your internships or co-ops will likely be the same. And that is the very reason why a future employer is more likely to hire you over someone else—someone who thought that a college education is confined to the classroom.

Highlight This: In the eyes of prospective employers, internship or co-op experience will separate you from other college students and recent grads who have other types of experience or, worse, no experience at all.

You Can Get Paid for an Unpaid Internship

Obstacles don't have to stop you. If you run into a wall, don't turn around and give up. Figure out how to climb it, go through it, or work around it.

Michael Jordan

It is one thing to think of an unpaid internship as a useful experience that "pays" in other ways—in the form of new skills you learn, for example, or new professional connections you make or new experiences to which you are exposed. But it is difficult to pay your credit card bill, buy dinner, or put gas in your car when the only currency you have is new skills, new professional connections, or new experiences. Oddly enough, your landlord wants a rent check each month and not a list featuring the intangible benefits you are getting from that unpaid internship of yours.

It is understandable, then, that you would be apt to quickly dismiss internship opportunities that do not offer at least a small stipend of some sort. In turning your back on these possibilities, though, you eliminate an awful lot of your internship options. And worse, you may be eliminating them unnecessarily, for you can sometimes find a way to get paid for an unpaid internship—or, more accurately, fund your unpaid internship using a backdoor strategy.

For example, some colleges and universities across the United States have set up special programs to help students who want to take unpaid internships but cannot afford to. At the University of Evansville (Indiana), for example, students can apply for internship stipends of up to $500. Similarly, Barnard College (New York) offers alumnae- and donor-sponsored internship grants ranging from $500 to $2,500.

Even if your school is one of the many that does not offer a special internship funding initiative, however, you can still explore several other options for getting the money you need to take the unpaid internship you really want:

Talk with a Financial Aid Counselor at Your School. Depending on your own or your family's income and circumstances, you may be eligible for financial aid in the form of grants or loans. It might sound a little crazy to, for instance, borrow extra money for a semester so that you can take on an unpaid internship. But if that internship ultimately leads to a paying job—one you may or may not have otherwise landed—then suddenly the extra loan money becomes not so much a debt as an investment in your future.

Get a Paying Job to Subsidize Your Internship. Many college students pay for their unpaid internships by working part time on the side in reasonably well-paying jobs like waiting tables (think tips) or shipping packages at a company like UPS or putting together lawn mower engines on an assembly line. You could also do occasional short-term stints with a temporary employment ("temp") agency. Is this path easy? Of course not. You might well find yourself working nights, weekends, or both for the short term. But if it helps you take on the unpaid internship that could very well lead to a permanent, full-time job in your field, isn't it worth at least considering?

Check into Outside Agencies Offering Grants, Scholarships, and Fellowships. Some professional and independent organizations offer special programs that can help you pay for educational experiences connecting closely to your career. The Harvard College Office of Career Services at Harvard University, for instance, publishes a handy compilation of such opportunities, *The Harvard College Guide to Grants*. Another good source is the book *Foundation Grants* *to Individuals*, published by the New York City–based Foundation Center.

Talk to Your Family and Relatives. More than one unpaid internship has been funded solely by the Bank of Mom and Dad.

Internship experience is too important to relinquish without a fight. So if the internship you want is unpaid, do not toss it into your "no way" pile just yet. You may be able to find another way to keep your checkbook nourished—so that you do not go hungry where internship experience is concerned.

Highlight This: You might be able to find the financial means to accept an unpaid internship. Do not give up on an unpaid internship without a fight.

Starting at the Bottom Is Not a Sadistic Hazing Ritual

Starting at the bottom is not about humiliation. It's about humility—a realistic assessment of where you are in the learning curve.

Maria Shriver

Nothing is more frustrating than being hired for an internship or even an entry-level job and then being assigned the types of tasks that your clueless seventh-grade brother could easily handle. "Why in the world," you might think as you make your umpteenth photocopy, "are they wasting my time and talents on this stuff when I could be doing things that are so much more important and valuable to the organization?"

It is a fair question—especially if your situation feels like some sort of test that is being thrust upon you by slightly higher-ups who themselves had to pass through the same ridiculous rite of passage before being allowed to don the title of true professional. "We all had to do this crap," you can almost hear them seething. "Now it's your turn."

It is true: Some of the mindless duties you will have as a newbie are assigned to you solely as secondhand payback by someone who had to do the same things when he or she was first hired. Feel free to be aggravated by these activities—for a minute or two. Once you are done, though, remind yourself that "starting at the bottom" has some valid purposes, too, both for you and for the organization:

You Have the Chance to Get Acclimated. Track athletes stretch and loosen up before their races so that they do not injure themselves—and so they give themselves the best chance of success once the starting gun sounds. Think of your newbie duties as the corporate equivalent of warming up. Far better to be under-whelmed at first and then work your way up to speed versus being overwhelmed at first and collapsing after the first lap.

You Learn the Basics of the Organization. In your interviews for the position, you undoubtedly learned quite a lot about the company, and your particular job, from a global standpoint. But you almost certainly did not get a feel for the nitty-gritty, everyday activities that make the company go. Somehow, some way, things get done in the organization each day. Some of those things are major; many are small-but-critical tasks that almost never emerge from their place behind the scenes. By giving you these types of tasks to complete, your new supervisor and co-workers do you the favor of opening your eyes to the many little pictures that make up the big picture.

You Discover Who Is Really Running the Organization. Who are the people that lead the organization? The people at the top, right? Not necessarily. Yes, the CEO runs the company on paper. But by doing some "grunt work," especially in the beginning, you will soon find out that many organizations—including yours, perhaps—would fail to function were it not for their skilled cus-tomer-service reps, administrative assistants, office managers, and others who do not get the glory (or the salary) the company president gets.

You Gain Credibility for the Future. Suppose one of your professional goals is to become a manager in your company's customer service department. At the moment, however, you are stuck making copies for one of the customer service reps. Your next gig—answering phones—is not much better. The company is wasting your time and talents, right? Wrong. Three years from now, when you are one of two finalists for the customer service manager position, who is the company going to hire: the outside candidate who has never actually worked in the customer service trenches, or you, who has—and who thus has not only the skills and experience but also, just as importantly, the credibility to be successful in the job?

In the classic movie *Animal House*, Kevin Bacon's character—the hopelessly naive Chip Diller—gets paddled on the butt by his fraternity brother, Doug Niedermeyer, during an initiation ceremony. Chip's repeated response: "Thank you, sir, may I have another?" You might feel like Chip Diller sometimes when you are new to a position and you are asked to complete tasks that seem beneath you. You need not respond with "Thank you, sir, may I have another?" But do keep in mind that, unlike Chip, you are not going through a sadistic hazing ritual; you are simply learning how to sweat the small stuff so that you can handle the much more difficult tasks and situations that will inevitably follow in the months ahead.

Highlight This: Starting at the bottom has a purpose: to prepare you for the middle and, eventually, the top.

Focus on Skills

Develop the Soft Skills Employers Demand

The typical interview process fixates on ensuring that new hires are technically competent. But coachability, emotional intelligence, motivation, and temperament are much more predictive of a new hire's success or failure.

Mark Murphy

Employers know that, if worse comes to worst, they can teach you the technical skills you have to know to be successful on the job. Need to learn the basics of HTML? A two-day course at the local community college will probably do the trick. Have you been asked—despite your lack of graphic design experience—to create a simple brochure for your nonprofit agency? A quick trip to the bookstore and an hour or two of reading will give you the essentials of effective visual communication.

But what if your *soft skills* are lacking? Suppose, for example, that you are less than reliable when it comes to completing assignments on time. Or maybe you have poor interpersonal skills. Or perhaps you do only what is asked of you—the bare minimum—and nothing more, no matter what unforeseen events might develop along the way. How can an employer take a chance on hiring you knowing that key traits and skills like integrity, self-motivation, and working well with others are nearly impossible to teach?

The short answer is that the employer cannot—and will not—take a chance on hiring you.

If you step back and think about it, this phenomenon only makes sense. You have probably done your share of group projects in college (and perhaps even in high school as well). Unless you have been incredibly fortunate, you have been teamed up along the way with at least one person whose soft skills were missing in action. You know who I am talking about. This is the person who showed up for a total of zero group meetings and then wondered why the rest of you stuck him with the work no one else wanted. This is the person who simply could not roll with the changes when you needed to add an important element to your group project at the last minute. This is the person who was a comedy legend in his own mind and took the opportunity during your group's class presentation to tell an insensitive joke that was hilarious only to him.

If you were an employer, would you hire this person for a job or an internship? No way. Thanks to his soft skills—or lack thereof—this guy is bad news in any group situation. He might be gifted enough to develop software that could take man to the moon and back, but since people cannot stand him, he will never be asked to write the first line of code—not for a job and a salary, at least!

Every year, the National Association of Colleges and Employers— a trade group made up of college career services professionals and employers that hire new college graduates—surveys its employer members about the soft skills they want to see in the college students they hire for entry-level jobs, internships, and co-ops. Year in and year out, the soft skills topping the list are basically the same:

Communication Skills. The rankings of the other most-sought-after soft skills fluctuate slightly from year to year, but communication skills—written and verbal—always head the list. You might be teeming with wonderful ideas. But if you cannot communicate those ideas effectively to other people—colleagues, clients, customers—you might as well not even have them in the first place.

Honesty and Integrity. Did you really interview all those people you quoted in the magazine article you just turned in to your editor? Are the numbers you collected from your recent lab experiment real or fiction? Employers cannot turn liars into truth tellers. So they make sure they do not hire liars to begin with.

Interpersonal Skills. Remember the line on your second-grade report card that said something to the effect of "works and plays well with others"? Hopefully, your teacher put a check mark on that line where you were concerned. Employers cannot—and will not—hire someone who will ultimately be despised by the rest of the employees in the organization.

Self-Motivation. Imagine yourself as an employer. You are considering two of your company's current interns for a full-time, permanent position that just opened up. One of these interns has the reputation of being a self-starter; he finds things that need doing and then does them. The other intern is known as someone who needs her hand held constantly and cannot even make coffee in the break room without asking for a go-ahead from her supervisor. In short, the first intern does things; the second waits to be told what to do. Who will you naturally end up hiring, thanks in no small part to his initiative?

Flexibility. No matter how hard any organization—large, small, or in between—tries to plan for anything and everything in advance, problems arise along the way. Plans change, and thus tasks must change along with them. Successful, well-regarded employees adapt and move forward. Floundering, hated employees throw hissy fits, dig in their heels, and screw things up thanks to their actions, their inactions, or both. Employers cannot send people to flexibility and adaptability training, though they undoubtedly wish they could at times. So unless you can demonstrate to a prospective employer that you are already flexible and adaptable, then you better have the flexibility to adapt to post-graduation life without a job.

You can develop the key soft skills you need to be a solid candidate in the eyes of future employers. Unfortunately, you will not be able to pull it off in an hour or a day or a week. Like a good steak, soft skills cook slowly. You need to start preparing them long before your postgraduation job search—in your classroom interactions, your extracurricular activities, your part-time jobs, your internships and co-ops, and your volunteer work. You may be the most intelligent, most technically capable person in the entire pool of candidates. But if you fail the soft skills test in an employer's eyes, you will be passed over for another candidate whose soft skills are well done—not rare or raw.

Highlight This: Your technical skills will not mean squat to prospective employers if you do not also have the soft skills necessary to thrive in today's team-oriented, ever-changing work environment.

Your Moneymaking Jobs Matter More Than You Think

Don't be afraid to give your best to what seemingly are small jobs. Every time you conquer one it makes you that much stronger. If you do the little jobs well, the big ones will tend to take care of themselves.

Dale Carnegie

It is true: The chances that an employer will hire you for a professional position solely because of your outstanding burger-flipping skills are somewhere in the neighborhood of zero. The same goes for your above-average ability to do your homework for an entire shift of your work-study job at the campus library, or to run the merry-go-round each summer at the local kiddie park.

During our college years, practically all of us take part-time jobs whose sole purpose is helping us make some extra money for school. Indeed, about 48 percent of today's students work to earn money for college, according to data from the National Center for Education Statistics, and the number is growing all the time as the cost of higher education goes up, up, up. Often these jobs seem mind-numbing at best and close to embarrassing at worst—certainly nothing to write home about when it comes to discussing your past work experience with prospective employers. "After all," you might think, "is anyone really going to be blown away by the fact that I cleaned up the biology lab twice a week?"

Probably not. But that does not mean your moneymaking jobs have no value at all in the minds of future employers. Experienced employers know better than to assume anything about any candidate for any job. Indeed, to an employer, your moneymaking job experiences offer evidence that:

Work Is Not a Foreign Concept to You. If you are under the impression that having a work ethic is a universal trait among college students—or anyone else, for that matter—you are badly mistaken. Some students do not and/or will not work. Period. You have seen these students. Remember that guy in your history class who did not follow through on his part of your group project, costing you and your teammates the A you were expecting? That is the guy a future employer does not want on the payroll. If you, on the other hand, can show an employer you have succeeded in several part-time moneymaking jobs, she can at least have some assurance that you are willing to work. She knows better than to assume it.

You Are Reliable. Believe it or not (it all depends on your experience), there are people in this world who have jobs but who choose to show up for work only when they feel like it. For some employees, a hot guest on *Oprah* is more than enough reason to stay home from work—without so much as a phone call to the boss. Granted, these folks do not last long in any job. But they are out there, and employers know it. So suddenly, the fact that you have overseen the miniature golf hut for three straight summers says something good about you—namely, that you are responsible and trustworthy enough for someone to hire you for three straight summers.

You Are Willing to Sacrifice. You may not have aspired to spend your summers hauling garbage to the local dump, or your spring break working nights at the local manufacturing plant. It does not matter. A future employer will look at that type of experience and rightly conclude, "Here's a person who seems willing to do less-than-pleasant things in order to achieve her higher goals." If you are an employer considering two new college graduates for an entry-level job, who are you going to believe—the one who *says* he is hardworking but has never worked, or the one who *shows* he is hardworking because he has worked hard?

You Are Flexible and Adaptable. Perhaps you had absolutely no idea how to make a latte under pressure until you had to learn this feat during your coffee shop job—with a long line of customers glaring at you. Maybe you had never worked with someone who did not look and talk just like you until you became a waiter at a local restaurant. Not everyone can jump right into a new situation and thrive. Ask any employer who has had to fire a new employee after a few days (or hours). Your moneymaking job experience may demonstrate nothing beyond your ability to go with the flow and fit in. These traits alone are huge in the mind of an employer.

If you were to rank their value to employers on a scale of one to ten—with ten being "extremely important" and one being "not at all important"—your moneymaking jobs would not be a ten—not even close. But they are not a one either! Treat them as the threes or fours they deserve to be—on your résumé and in your interviews with prospective employers. They add up to critical skills and traits that employers are not foolish enough to take for granted.

Highlight This: The skills and traits you develop in your moneymaking jobs matter more to future employers than you might think. You may not land a postgraduation job solely because you have these skills and traits, but you will definitely lose out on postgraduation opportunities if you do not have them.

Campus Activities Build Essential Skills That You May Overlook

Being valuable to an organization in college will teach you how to become valuable to a company.

Carol Carter

When I was an undergraduate at Moorhead State University in Minnesota, I worked for two years as a disc jockey at the campus radio station, KMSC. This job was not exactly glamorous. None of us DJs was paid for our, ahem, talents. It was strictly a volunteer gig. We did it as much for the access to free records and the occasional brush with greatness (singer Richard Marx once stopped by) as the radio experience. Worse, no one listened to KMSC. I mean that quite literally; no one—as in zero students—listened to the station. For starters, AM radio was not exactly impressive to students who were accustomed to blasting heavy metal songs out of their residence hall window speakers. Worse, KMSC's signal was not a signal at all. The station did not go out over the airwaves. It was fed to the campus residence halls via wires—real, physical wires—and even then you could only pick the station up intermittently.

Let me put it this way: You know no one is listening to you when you are on the air offering a free hit record to the *first* person who calls and the phone never rings. (This happened routinely on my watch, often during the middle of the day when students were actually walking by the station's offices and could hear me on the loudspeaker—if they had been listening, that is!)

Perhaps you have had—or you will have—similar experiences with the activities and organizations you are involved with on campus. Are you wasting your time and energy? Not likely. As I look back on my KMSC experiences, for example, as well as several other campus activities I pursued (including the student senate and the student newspaper), I can see now what I wish I had spotted when I graduated from college in 1990 and began looking for a job in what was then a slumping economy—namely, the fact that most campus activities give you the chance to develop several essential skills and traits that are important to prospective employers:

Passion and Dedication. The vast majority of campus activities pay nothing. (I know I certainly was not involved in KMSC for the riches.) And even those that do usually pay a pittance. I remember being paid for my student newspaper articles, for example: one dollar per column-inch. So if you join and get involved in a student organization or some other campus activity, you are probably doing so out of sheer interest. Employers understand that—and they are impressed by it.

Leadership. The term *leadership* is tossed around so much that it is difficult to understand what it really means anymore. But viewed through the lens of campus activities, leadership evolves naturally when you participate in tasks like raising money for a group or a cause, recruiting members to a group or a cause, organizing successful events, and even running meetings effectively so that they do not turn into one- or two-hour naps or screw-around fests for participants.

Interpersonal Skills. When my friend Monte Rogneby was president of the student senate during my time at Moorhead State, he met regularly with the president of the university. Monte had great interpersonal skills going into the job; he had even better interpersonal skills when it was over. You may not have the chance to meet with your school's president when you are involved in campus activities. But perhaps you will invite a local professional to speak to your group, or maybe you will need to convince a faculty member to become your group's adviser. Whatever the scenario, you will improve your interpersonal skills in the process.

Written Communication Skills. The typical student organization has to put in a funding request each year, which is then considered by a group of student leaders who allocate student-fee money. Do you want your group to get as much funding as possible? Then you had better be able to write up a solid argument for it. Similarly, you may have to write recruiting-oriented content for your group's Web site, or perhaps take on an even higher-level project by collaborating on the text of a bill that you would like a state legislator to propose during an upcoming session. You will improve your writing skills along the way; if you do not, you will probably be unsuccessful in your efforts.

Keep in mind, too, that you might also develop skills essential to the specific future career you have in mind. At KMSC, for instance, I learned how to write and produce 30-second radio ads that included music and a voice-over—not a bad experience for a guy who ultimately ended up working in another communications field, publishing. Maybe you want to go into public relations someday—event coordination in particular. If you work with a group of your fellow students to bring a top band to campus for an outdoor concert, presto: suddenly you have proven experience in key tasks like securing a venue, negotiating with entertainers and their reps, identifying and addressing liability issues, overseeing safety and security, and evaluating what went well and what did not.

I still remember my time at KMSC with a smile. Yes, it would have been nice if someone besides me had laughed at my, um, witty banter all those years ago. But the confidence I gained on the air ensured I would be heard—eventually—when I graduated and entered the world of work. Your campus activities are teaching you similar skills. Are you paying attention?

Highlight This: Though your involvement in campus activities probably will not pay you anything from a financial standpoint, you will earn plenty in the form of skills and traits that will impress prospective employers someday.

Your Classroom Experiences Matter to Employers

The classroom should be an entrance into the world, not an escape from it.

John Ciardi

No matter what your major, the courses you take in college can play a surprisingly decisive role in your landing a job or an internship—not so much because of their content or the grades you earn, but because of the key skills and traits you develop in the typical college classroom over the course of two or four years.

Now, let's be clear as well as realistic: Will an employer ever ask you when the Treaty of Versailles was signed and why? Probably not. Will a company internship coordinator base her hiring decision on your ability to balance chemical equations or describe the path of a bill as it moves through Congress? Unlikely. But that does not mean employers are not interested in your classroom performance and activities. Indeed, if you devote just a little time and energy to identifying your key academic experiences and what you learned from them, you will almost certainly be able to add several compelling items to the list of skills and traits you can market to prospective employers.

As you reflect upon your classroom experiences of the last few years, think in particular about:

Group Activities and Projects. One of the most common questions employers ask in interviews these days goes something like this:

Tell me about a time when you were working with a group of people and one of those people was not carrying his or her weight.

This type of question is known as a *behavioral* question, and its intent is to help the employer understand not what you *would do* in a hypothetical situation, but what you *have done* in that actual situation in the past. If you have done any group projects in your classes—as most of today's college students have—you might well be able to relate the difficulties you had with a particular team member during one of these projects. You will have a real story—a situation you can describe, the actions you took, and the results—that will serve as a solid response to the employer's question.

Moreover, if you and your group had to develop and deliver a class presentation connected to your project, you will be able to tell employers—on paper and in person—not only how you put the content together but also how you gained firsthand experience sharing the stage with several other presenters. You will likely be doing the same thing in any job or internship you pursue; you and a few colleagues might be asked, for example, to take on a project and share your findings or results with the rest of the staff.

Research You Conducted. Many college courses, especially at the upper levels, require you to put together lengthy research papers. At a minimum, you will boost your information-gathering, analytical, and writing skills as you complete these tasks. But every once in a while you will be asked—or required—to take on an even bigger project. Edgewood College in Wisconsin, for example—where I used to work as a counselor—requires all students to design and complete a Human Issues project. Students at other institutions must write a senior thesis or complete a senior seminar. These ventures and others like them are demanding by their very scope and depth, practically forcing you to hone key skills like identifying an intriguing or unaddressed issue, narrowing the focus of that issue to a manageable level, perhaps conducting original research, writing up your findings, and presenting those finding to your faculty adviser or a group from the campus community. Employers will not know about your project or what you learned from it, however, unless and until you take the initiative to talk about it.

Technical or Computer Skills You Developed. If you are like many college students, you are prone to downplaying your computer skills (see **Do Not Take Your Technology Skills for Granted**, p. 174). But thanks to your classroom activities, you might well be ahead of more-experienced workers when it comes to technical matters: using spreadsheet data to generate eye-catching charts and graphs, for example, or creating PowerPoint slides for presentations, or using search engines and online databases to gather difficult-to-find information.

Sure, you can probably permanently shelve the in-depth knowledge of ocean clams you gained on your way to a B+ in Biology 101. But do not overlook—among many other things—the teamwork skills you gained during the dissection labs, the research skills you developed when you studied why ocean clams are endangered in some parts of the world, and the presentation skills you gained as you and your partners shared your newfound knowledge with professor and peers alike. Your classroom experiences matter more than you think—to you and to prospective employers.

Highlight This: While your future job may not require you to regurgitate specific knowledge you are learning in your classes, it will almost certainly tap many of the associated skills and traits you are developing through your course-related activities.

Volunteer for Your Career

The nonprofessional volunteer world is a laboratory for self-realization.

Madeleine Kunin

I owe my career to volunteering.

In the fall of 1995, I was just a few courses into my master's program at the University of Wisconsin-Whitewater. At the time I did not really know what I was going to do with my counseling degree upon graduation in 1998. All I knew, as I kept telling my wife over and over again, was that I wanted to help people. That mantra had been my entire reason for going to graduate school—not the greatest reason, I will admit, but not the worst either—and I was determined to carry it out, eventually, in my career. I just did not know how—until opportunity showed up in the form of an announcement one of my instructors made in class.

The school's career center, it turned out, was looking for volunteers—graduate students as well as undergraduates—to lead *career planning groups* for freshmen and sophomores who were struggling to decide what to major in and what career to ultimately pursue. All volunteers would go through an extensive training program and then team up with coleaders to work with small groups of students for two hours a week, six weeks straight.

I was immediately intrigued, in great part because of my own career struggles. "In some ways," I thought to myself at the time, "I'm a horrible candidate for this job; I can't even get my own career stuff right!" But another voice inside of me was arguing just the opposite: "Who better to empathize with people who are struggling with their careers than someone who has also struggled with his?" Fortunately, the second voice won the debate, and I applied to become a career planning group leader. I was both thrilled and terrified when I actually landed one of the positions. But before long, my emotions turned to love—for as soon as our training sessions began, I just knew I had somehow found my way home. When our sessions with the students began, my passion only grew stronger.

My supervisor at the time, Gail Fox, noticed my passion for the career planning groups. So she encouraged me the following year to apply for a paid graduate assistantship position in the career center. I got it. And I got it again the following year. In fact, by the time that last year rolled around, I was working in or for the career center—either as a paid graduate assistant, an unpaid practicum student (part of my graduate program requirements), or an unpaid career planning group leader—more than 30 hours a week. Thus, thanks to a volunteer activity emerging out of a class announcement that I easily could have missed or slept through or ignored, I finished graduate school with the equivalent of about two years of semiprofessional career services experience.

More importantly, I found my new career—one I continue to love today.

By definition, you do not make any money as a volunteer. But if you think volunteering does not pay at all, then you have to reexamine your definition of "pay." As I have discovered through my own experiences as well as the experiences of people I have counseled, the salary you earn for volunteering comes not only in what you contribute to the cause you are volunteering for but also in the:

Skills You Learn and/or Develop. Perhaps you are a decent public speaker but you want to get even better at it. By becoming a volunteer tour guide for your school's admissions office, you can practice over and over and over again, in front of both prospective students and their parents. Would you like to learn a brand-new skill—Web design, for instance? Why not check into a volunteer Web development position at a local nonprofit agency?

Career Interests You Uncover. I can easily make myself crazy by imagining what I would be doing now had I not heard—and responded to—that in-class announcement about career planning group volunteers at UW-Whitewater all those years ago. I may never have discovered how passionate I am about career development issues, and I certainly would never have made a career out of that passion. Think about the passions you might discover by simply donating a few hours of your time, energy, and attention.

Professional Connections You Make. Gail Fox became an almost instant mentor to me at UW-Whitewater, as did her supervisor, Carolyn Gorby, and her colleague, Jerry McDonald. It was not long before Gail and Carolyn in particular were pulling me aside and telling me, "Now, Peter, you make sure you join the Wisconsin Career Planning and Placement Association"—the professional group they were both heavily involved in—"and start attending the conferences with us." I did, and before long, I knew other career services professionals around the state of Wisconsin. I set up an informational interview with one of them, George Heideman of Edgewood College in Madison, who ultimately invited me to do part of my counseling practicum at Edgewood, and who later hired me for my first post-graduate-school job in counseling.

Volunteer opportunities are easy to find: Just visit your school's career or volunteer and service-learning center, get in touch with your local United Way chapter, or visit the Web site VolunteerMatch (http://www.volunteermatch.org), which allows you to search for volunteer opportunities by simply typing in your zip code. You will not make any money in your volunteer activities. But you will most definitely get paid.

Highlight This: Volunteering will help you develop the skills and connections you will need to land a paying job after graduation.

Identify the Skills You Have Gained from Hobbies and Avocations

My object in living is to unite my avocation with my vocation, as my two eyes make one in sight.

Robert Frost

Your marketable skills come from your *entire* life, not just the life you lead in class or during your internship or even participating in a student organization on campus. We all have lives outside of our, well, lives; specifically, we all have hobbies or *avocations* that help us build essential skills—though it usually happens behind the scenes, without our being aware of it.

Suppose, for example, that you are a philosophy major who also enjoys buying and selling products of all kinds on eBay. None of it has anything to do with your major or your future career aspiration of becoming a book editor for a college press—or so you might think. But wait a minute—you are overlooking the many skills you are learning through your eBay-related activities:

Technical Skills. Buying and selling stuff on eBay is not rocket science. But you do need to have some basic technical skills to pull it off. You have to set up an eBay account, for starters, and then learn how to buy items from others, and especially how to sell items to others. It all requires a certain comfort level with the Internet and the Web, not to mention the willingness and ability to read, understand, and follow technical directions that send many people running for another hobby.

Presentation Skills. The people who have the most success selling on a site like eBay are invariably the people who do the best job of presenting the products they have for sale. That includes writing compelling copy and—far too often overlooked—taking good pictures of their products instead of throwing up a blurry, poorly lit snapshot or two.

Pricing Strategies. With experience, you begin to understand what is realistic when you are setting your minimum product prices. You also begin to understand what various items are worth—and why—by simply watching pricing and buying trends over time.

Entrepreneurship. By its nature—indeed, by its very existence—a Web site like eBay draws and demands people who have an entrepreneurial streak. After all, you could be doing something else with your time, energy, and money if you wanted to; but you have chosen to devote at least some of those resources to buying and/or selling products online.

Will any of these skills come in handy to you when you are approaching hiring managers at college presses to compete for a book-editing job? Of course! To wit:

- You will need to be able to demonstrate solid *technical skills* to anyone working for any publishing company, particularly if you are involved in tasks like editing manuscripts or laying out copy. You will need your technical skills for activities like research and fact checking, too.

- Your *presentation skills* will be essential when you send out résumés and cover letters and, later, when you have interviews. Once you are on the job as a college press editor, you will almost certainly be at least tangentially involved in tasks like cover design and the design of a book's inside text. You might also end up attending publishing trade shows, where you will be required to set up your college press's books in a way that compels attendees to stop by your booth and have a look.

- If you understand *pricing strategies* thanks to your eBay experiences, then you will know the basics of pricing where books are concerned too. You will know that a book's price is not just snatched out of thin air; it is based on a variety of key factors, such as production costs, distribution costs, marketing costs, and market demand.

- If the college press you work for is like many these days, it is struggling financially. As such, it is constantly looking for new books, new markets, and new authors. (Yes, many college presses are nonprofit operations; but they still need money to survive.) If you have a predisposition to *entrepreneurship*—thanks in part to your eBay experiences—you will be that much more appealing to the hiring manager of a financially stressed college press.

Will the skills you develop through your hobbies and avocations land you a job all by themselves? Not likely. But that does not mean they do not count—or that they are not valuable. They will not count or be valuable, however, unless you count and place value on them yourself.

Highlight This: Identify the skills you are developing through your various hobbies and avocations. Some of them might well be of interest to prospective employers—but not if you never discuss them!

Do Not Take Your Technology Skills for Granted

I would rather be able to appreciate things I cannot have than to have things I am not able to appreciate.

Elbert Hubbard

I will never forget a sign I once saw at an agency where my wife was working. It was a set of detailed instructions—describing how to turn on the computer.

At the publishing company where I used to work, I was once asked to show one of the new editors how to use the computer. I was rendered speechless when she picked up the mouse—as in she held it in the air—and pointed it at the computer screen, figuring (I guess) that it must work like a TV remote or a phaser from *Star Trek*.

Several of the teachers at my son's preschool are too fearful to check their e-mail, to say nothing of sending new e-mails themselves.

I don't bring up these examples to make fun of anyone. I just want you to know something that you probably do not know right now: The "basic" computer and technology skills you use every day of your life as a college student—e-mail, cell phone, instant messaging, word processing, and all the rest—baffle or even scare a significant portion of America's working population. Surprisingly, the problem is relatively widespread. And it is not confined only to "older" people in their forties, fifties, and sixties.

When you are a college student or recent graduate, it is easy to think that veteran workers are ahead of you in every way—that you simply cannot compete with, let alone beat, their skills and experience. Well, guess what: Chances are you can outshine experienced workers when it comes to computer and technology skills.

To you, finding industry or company information is as simple as a few well-chosen key words or phrases on Google—a process that allows you to quickly and easily uncover current and compelling data. But to someone who has been in the workforce for a while and who does not have your computer skills, finding industry or company information is a matter of digging through yellowing paper files—a process that painstakingly leads to outdated and irrelevant data.

To you, keeping track of important industry contacts is a matter of setting up a simple Microsoft Access database, or perhaps going even simpler and using the Address Book tool in Microsoft Outlook. But to someone who has been in the workforce for a while and who does not have your computer skills, keeping track of important industry contacts involves misplacing—and ultimately losing—people's business cards.

To you, calculating the cost of a marketing mailing involves developing a spreadsheet that automatically updates itself, in a split second, every time you enter new or updated data. To someone who has been in the workforce for a while and who does not have your computer skills, calculating the cost of a marketing mailing involves recalculating the numbers by hand—over and over and over again as those numbers change.

In most key skill and experience areas, veteran employees can most likely outperform you; you probably have no business claiming otherwise. But when it comes to computers and technology, you have a rare chance to show up the veterans—and, perhaps more importantly, to point out this disparity to potential employers and offer yourself as a solution. Here are some tasks for which your comfort with technology will likely give you an edge:

Research. Today's organizations know how critical information is to their continued existence. Indeed, many companies go so far as to hire information-gathering gurus as *competitive intelligence* experts. You may not have reached "guru" status when it comes to research, but if you have become adept at using electronic databases like Lexis/Nexis, ProQuest, and Academic Search Premier—by using them to gather information for your routine academic papers, for example, or for something more substantial like a senior thesis—you can sell that comparatively rare proficiency to prospective employers.

Troubleshooting. You are going to encounter people in the world of work who practically run away from their computers screaming if, for example, Microsoft Word does something funky on them while they are typing a document. You will also run into people who will decide to make their photocopies later—or not at all—rather than attempt to fix the paper jam, as well as people who will continue trying to print on the network laser printer even when nothing is coming out. (These are the people who wonder what is going on when dozens of copies of the same document eventually spew forth from the printer after the problem has been fixed.) If you are willing and able to handle even the most basic technological troubleshooting, you can sell that skill to an employer. That employer knows who the technophobes are in his or her organization. (Sometimes it is the person the employer sees in the mirror each day.)

Improving Efficiency. One of the greatest problems in any organization is the phenomenon of "we've always done it this way." Sheer momentum and lack of awareness will compel people in an organization to do things inefficiently at times. I have been guilty of many such inefficiencies myself. I once had an intern whose job, in part, was to type people's names and addresses into a form letter I had developed. She did not come right out and put it this way, but essentially she said to me one day, "Hey, ever hear of the mail merge tool in Word?" She then proceeded to cut the time needed to complete this task by probably 90 percent or more. We all have our efficiency-related blind spots, and often they are just a technological step or two away from being addressed. You could be the one to help a prospective employer see how something can be done—and done better—using technology.

If you are like many college students and recent graduates, you probably see your technological skills as merely average. Perhaps that is true where your peer group is concerned. But in the world of work, there is a good chance your average skills rise to the level of good or even superior when compared to those of your older colleagues. So do not take your technology skills for granted. Pinpoint them. Acknowledge them. And then market them.

Highlight This: The technological skills and tools that are routine or easy for you are often anything but routine and easy for older, more experienced employees.

PART IV

LAND THE JOB
YOU REALLY WANT

Introduction

Think Like an Employer, Win the Job

Seek first to understand, then to be understood.

Stephen Covey

For years I have had a vision for a job-search workshop that I would call *Job Hunting as an Out-of-Body Experience*. I have never bothered to follow through with the idea, though, because I know what people would think: "out-of-body experience"—hmm, this guy has been watching too much late-night TV. I do watch a lot of late-night TV, but I am not talking about "crossing over to the other side" to discuss job-hunting strategies with ghosts or other residents of The Great Beyond. My vision is, in fact, much more down to earth and easier to understand. All you have to do is think of shoes—as in "put yourself in the employer's shoes." If you can achieve that one single feet—er, feat—you will do more for your job search than you could any other way.

Try it right now: Imagine leaving your body and putting yourself in the shoes of the hiring manager for Company X, who oversees the recruitment of recent college graduates for entry-level jobs at the company. It is spring—the height of the entry-level hiring season for Company X—and you are busy doing all sorts of things. But never mind what you are doing; how are you feeling right now? Here is a brief rundown. You are probably:

Strapped for Time. If Company X is like most businesses, the people there, including you, are being asked to do too much with too few resources. Spring recruiting season is just one of these situations where you are concerned. You are working 50- and sometimes 55-hour weeks, but you still cannot finish everything you need to get done. (Occasionally those long weeks are putting a strain on your personal life.) Among dozens of other things, you have a stack of résumés on your desk (or in your e-mail box, as the case may be) and a full slate of interviews with college seniors over the next three weeks.

Under Pressure. Every time Company X hires a great college senior who goes on to be a huge success with the organization, the credit seems to go to someone else. Aggravating! But every time Company X makes a bad hire from the graduating class of college seniors, the CEO's finger points to you and your staff. Before all is said and done, each poor hiring decision ends up costing the company nearly $10,000 in wasted recruiting costs alone. You know it; the CEO *really* knows it. The pressure is on for you and your staff to get it right—every single time.

Skeptical Until a Candidate Proves You Should Not Be. The last college senior who turned into a bad hire absolutely killed in his interview. You were dazzled by him and so was everyone else the student talked to. Unfortunately, you had to let him go after only four months on the job. Everything he had said in his interviews had turned out to be a performance worthy of an Oscar. "We won't be fooled again" has become your internal and external rallying cry.

Now step back into your own shoes as a job candidate. Are you surprised by what the employer version of you was thinking and feeling and why? Don't be. The employers you will be dealing with from here on out will undoubtedly be friendly with you, and they will certainly be hoping they can hire you and thus be one step closer to meeting their organizations' hiring needs. No one wants to interview people indefinitely, after all. But the more you can get into their heads, or their shoes, or their bodies, or [insert your own metaphor here], and act according to their thoughts and feelings, the better the chance you will be chosen for the position over one of your competitors.

What exactly can you do to conduct yourself in a way that will grab—and hold—the attention of the busy, stressed, skeptical-bordering-on-cynical employer?

Save Her Time. Keep both your cover letter and your résumé to a page each if at all possible. No, it is not "required" (as much as you might hear that it is). But concise documents—ones that are also well designed—are documents that an employer can scan quickly to get what she needs.

Does the advertisement for the position you are applying for say something like "No phone calls, please"? Then do not call the employer to follow up after you have sent in your cover letter and résumé! Conversely, if there is no admonition against following up and you decide to do so with, say, a phone call, keep it brief—to a couple of minutes at most.

Show Her You Want *Her* Job at *Her* Company—Not Just *Any* Job at *Any* Company. Imagine yourself as an employer again. You have the cover letters of two college seniors in front of you. The one on the left is clearly the same cover letter the applicant has sent to dozens or even hundreds of other companies—the ultimate generic letter. The one on the right, conversely, is clearly customized for *you* and the job *you* have open at *your company*. You can tell because the applicant briefly mentions an article she saw about your company in last week's local newspaper. She also includes a sentence about how the work she's doing in her current internship would help her contribute to the launch of a new product your division is coming out with in the next year.

Which applicant wants *your* job at *your company*? And therefore which applicant will you bring in for an interview?

Back Up Any and All Claims You Make. Why in the world should the employer take anything you say—whether in writing or in person—at face value? (Remember: Last time she did that, she got burned by the applicant who was hired and then quickly fired.) She won't. She will be looking for proof that you actually have the skills, education, and experience you claim to have. If you are savvy enough to offer such evidence—and you then ultimately provide it—you will soar past the other candidates for the position.

Step back into the employer's chair just one last time. You are interviewing candidates for an entry-level public relations job that involves a lot of professional writing—news releases, Web site content, newsletter articles, and the like. Candidate A comes in and says she could handle all of those activities. You ask her if she has any published samples of her writing that you could take a look at. "I didn't think to bring any," she replies. A half-hour later, you are interviewing Candidate B. You ask her the same question about published writing samples, but you already know what the answer is going to be—for you can plainly see the portfolio she has brought with her to the interview. Out it comes. The student then proceeds to show you dozens of news articles she has written for her campus newspaper over the last two years. She also shows you the news releases she wrote during her summer internship at her school's university relations office.

Candidate A might well be right in her self-assessment, but all she has to back it up is talk. Candidate B did not need to say a word; she showed you everything you needed to know. Who gets the job?

In his best-selling book *The 7 Habits of Highly Effective People* (Simon & Schuster, 1989), author Stephen Covey's fifth habit is: "Seek First to Understand, Then to Be Understood." Apply that advice—if only that advice alone—to your job search and the next set of shoes you will be stepping into are the ones you buy for the new job you just accepted.

Perfect Your Attitude

Entitlement Kills

Don't be misled into believing that somehow the world owes you a living.

David Sarnoff

If you are an employer and you read enough articles about the Millennial Generation—the current group of Generation Y college twentysomethings born in the late 1970s or early to mid-1980s—you will come away thinking the entire generation can be broadly described in one ugly word: *entitled*. Entitled to acceptance into the best school(s) before college, entitled to high-quality education and opportunities during college, and entitled to great jobs immediately after college. Entitled to this and entitled to that without having to suffer any hardships along the way.

Your negative attitude toward Gen Yers grows even worse when you meet an internship or job candidate who seems to be a walking billboard for the annoying Gen Y stereotype. In an article in the *Chicago Tribune*, an employer expressed her dismay about the intern her organization had hired who immediately asked if she could do all of her work from home. The employer could not believe what she was hearing and told the newspaper: "I think there is in some ways a sense of entitlement that these young workers are so valuable that they should not be demeaned by being asked to do administrative or menial tasks."

Are all members of the Millennial Generation spoiled brats who are unwilling to work hard and prove themselves to employers before reaping rewards like higher salaries and better opportunities? Of course not—and you have every right to be angry at that

186 Career Wisdom for College Students

assessment if you are a Gen Yer yourself. (I know I certainly get tired of hearing about how my own Generation X is made up of tens of millions of "slackers" who care only about themselves.) But here is the problem: For better or worse, many of the employers out there now *perceive* you and your fellow Millennials to be people who do indeed view themselves as entitled to the best—and entitled to it immediately—where your careers are concerned.

"If you're a Gen Y student, you need to adopt the attitude 'guilty until proven innocent' where employers' perceptions of you and the attitude of entitlement are concerned," says Terese Corey Blanck, director of student development for Roseville, Minnesota, internship company Student Experience (http://www.studentexperience.com), which hires college students as personal care assistants (PCAs) for clients with disabilities. "Your fellow recent Gen Y grads have paved a path that has made potential employers look at the glass as half empty where Gen Yers are concerned."

Is this fair? No. Is it right? No. But as 18th-century philosopher Immanuel Kant once said, "Perception is reality." What you see as unjust generalization, an employer might view as a perfectly legitimate and accurate way of viewing the typical Gen Y candidate. Whether employers are reading about Gen Y in their professional journals, discussing Gen Y at their professional conferences, or hearing stories about Gen Y on the radio or TV, they are often coming to believe that you and your fellow Gen Yers:

- Are unwilling to start at the bottom and work your way up.

- Are prone to needing constant hand-holding and positive feedback on how you are doing.

- Constantly question how organizations do things and why.

- Cannot communicate effectively face-to-face (versus using e-mail or instant messaging).

- Immediately want perks like more vacation time or work-from-home flexibility, even when older employees have had to work for years or even decades to get them.

- Care only about your own growth and development and not that of the company or organization.

- Are averse to grunt work that most everyone in the organization has to do (e.g., photocopying, making coffee, taking out your office garbage).

- Are unable to make difficult decisions on your own or deal with ambiguity versus right or wrong "answers."

During your job search, then, you will be paying for the sins of some of the Gen Yers who have gone before you. Many of the employers you approach will assume the worst about you as a Millennial candidate until they have solid reasons to assume something better. You have to give them those reasons—loudly and clearly. Here's how:

Address the Stereotypes Head-On. In your cover letter, for example, you can subtly tell the employer that you are aware of her potential fears about you as a Gen Yer, and that she need not be afraid. For example:

> The other candidates who approach you for this position may give the impression that they are out only for themselves, or that they are unwilling to work hard to prove themselves to you. Please know that just the opposite is true in my case—and I am prepared to demonstrate that to you in an interview. I am not the "entitled" Gen Yer you read about in the paper!

Highlight Not Only What You *Can Do*, but Also What *You Have Already Done*. Every job candidate talks a good game about what he or she can do or will do for a particular employer. (No one ever writes in a cover letter, for example, "I really have nothing to offer you" or "I'm not going to try very hard"!) But if you want to be the rare (in the employer's eyes) Gen Y candidate who defies the "entitled" stereotype, show the employer what you have already done that makes you a solid candidate for the job. It is difficult for an employer to overlook a Gen Y candidate who does not simply say she is committed to her chosen field, but shows it through her previous activities and accomplishments, on and off campus.

Back Up Your Claims with Solid Evidence. A professor or supervisor who can tell employers about your commitment to carefully researching a topic before moving forward will carry much more weight than you yourself saying, "I am committed to researching a topic carefully before moving forward." Your involvement first as an active member and then as treasurer and then as elected president of your student organization says far more about your willingness to work your way up than does your job interview claim, "I am willing to work my way up."

You might be the exact opposite of the Gen Y stereotype. But many employers will peg you as a "typical Millennial" who wants the world and wants it now—and they will go out of their way to deny it to you. You have to prove them wrong, stresses Corey Blanck. How? By adopting a slightly modified version of the philosophy touted by John F. Kennedy in his 1961 inauguration speech: "Ask not what the company can do for you; ask what you can do for the company."

Highlight This: If you are a member of the Millennial Generation (Generation Y), you can be sure that most employers will assume the worst about you. It will be up to you to prove that you do not feel "entitled" to a job or to the opportunities a job offers.

'Give Me a Chance' Will Give You No Chance

Life is not divided into semesters. You don't get summers off, and very few employers are interested in helping you find yourself.

Bill Gates

In his book *Jobs That Don't Suck: What Nobody Else Will Tell You About Getting and Succeeding in the Job of Your Dreams* (Ballantine Books, 1998), author Charlie Drozdyk offers a blunt, yet eloquent reminder of how jobs come to be:

> A job is a product of somebody's hard work and inability to do everything on their own. For example, say Jill and Jane start a design company out of their living room. They max out their credit cards and eat peanut butter sandwiches for two years before they start making money. Their hard work pays off, and now they have more clients and more work than they can handle on their own. They take a look at their books and decide they can **just** afford to hire somebody to take up the extra load of work. … This is what a job is. … They're dipping into **their** profits to give **you** a job.

Talk to practically any entrepreneur and you will soon see the Energizer Bunny emerge before you. Most people who start companies would *love* to do *everything* in those companies if they could. But at some point that becomes impossible; there is too much to be done and too few people to do it. So employees are hired. The company grows some more, and more employees are hired. Then the company grows even more, and so on and so on and so on.

When you are in college—or even further along in your professional life, for that matter—it is easy to fall into the trap of believing that jobs simply *are*. You might think of the jobs of the world in much the same way you view candy bars at the convenience store: You go in, you proceed to the candy aisle, you look at the dozens or even hundreds of options that are just magically sitting there, you pick the one you want, you plunk your money on the counter, and you start munching away as you walk out to your car. But jobs *aren't* candy bars, or oranges, or options on the menu of a Chinese restaurant. In the mind of an employer, jobs are a necessary evil— the activities the founder of the company might well be handling herself if the idea was not so preposterous. And jobs are not handed out to just anyone who stops by with 69 cents in hand; jobs go to people who can earn their salaries back—and then some—for the organization.

One of the most frequent questions I get from college students and recent graduates goes something like this:

> I feel I have a lot to offer an employer. But I don't have any experience. Employers expect you to have experience, but you need a job to get that experience! Why aren't any employers willing to *give me a chance*?

The answer—from the employer's standpoint, at least—is simple and straightforward: Employers are not in business to "give chances"; they are in business to be as successful as they possibly can, and the only way they can do that is to hire the best people they can find. Period.

A while back a colleague and I gave a job-search presentation to a group of people who had recently been laid off from their positions. As I talked about how employers think when it comes to jobs and filling those jobs, I got into a fairly intense exchange with one young audience member who brought up the "why won't employers give me a chance?" question for discussion. I asked her to put herself in an employer's shoes for a minute and to imagine herself trying to decide between two candidates for a job: one who was clearly *offering* something to her and her small company and another who was subtly asking for "a chance." The young woman surprised me by saying she would offer the job to the latter candidate—because she could relate to that candidate given her own precarious employment situation.

"But what if," I countered, "this company was really *your* company? What if you'd mortgaged your own home to get it going and failure would mean losing everything you have? Would you still give the job to the candidate who wants 'a chance'?"

"Yes," she said firmly.

"I'm sorry," I replied, "but, respectfully, I just don't buy that. If your house was *really* on the line and you *really* could lose everything, you'd hire the best person for the job."

The woman never did budge—despite the gentle but real scoffs she began to hear from others in the audience—but I didn't either. Why? Because employers will not—and do not—hire people they perceive to be beggars or whiners or charity cases. They do not hire candidates who are *asking for* something; they hire candidates who are *offering* something.

So eliminate the "why won't employers give me a chance?" attitude from your job search mind-set. It is perfectly fine—and understandable—to feel that type of frustration on your own time. But if it seeps into your interactions with employers, "give me a chance" will give you no chance of succeeding.

Highlight This: When given the choice, an employer will hire the candidate who is offering something over the candidate who wants something—every time.

Yes, You *Do* Have Contacts to Network With!

A hidden connection is stronger than an obvious one.

Heraclitus of Ephesus

A few years ago, some typical students at a typical university in a typical Wisconsin town taught me a lesson that was anything but typical.

A colleague and I were delivering a networking presentation at the University of Wisconsin-River Falls, a midsize school that is similar to thousands of other comprehensive institutions across the United States. We began our seminar with what turned out to be an eye-opening exercise: We took a large ball of yarn and asked each of the dozen or so students in the room to name one person they knew who held some sort of interesting job. After each student identified someone, he or she tossed the ball of string to the next student, ultimately creating a web of yarn that visually demonstrated how "we are all connected."

Going into the seminar, I really had not known what to expect from this activity. My only hope was that it would show the students that networking does not have to be difficult, and that people they already knew could be helpful to them in their networking efforts. The exercise was a success in that regard. But the real lesson—the more profound one—surprised everyone in the room, including me. For in this small group of 12 everyday, average college students in the upper Midwest, there were direct connections to people who could pave the way to extraordinary opportunities:

- One student's family was friends with Casey FitzRandolph, the 2002 Olympic gold medalist in 500-meter speed skating. This same student had worked for several years for the local Chamber of Commerce, where he had met dozens of people working in a variety of diverse fields.

- Another student's family knew former Wisconsin Governor Tommy Thompson, who would later become the U.S. Secretary of Health and Human Services. In fact, the student pointed out, "[Thompson] told me that if I ever needed any help in my job or internship search, I should let him know."

- One of the two UW-River Falls career counselors in the room knew someone who reviewed the résumés of college students who applied for internships with the U.S. Department of State.

- Another student had an aunt who worked in sales and traveled throughout Europe as part of her job.

- Still another student was going to be traveling to Belize with one of his archaeology professors, who had considerable connections in that field.

One of the most common networking questions I hear from college students is, "How do I network when I have no one to network *with*?" I always pull out this story to prove to them that they do have people they can—and should—tap to learn about job possibilities. Indeed, often the people who can help you the most in your networking activities are so close to you that you do not even see them. So as you search for that first real job after graduation, be sure you tap the four sets of people most often overlooked by college students and recent grads:

Your Fellow Students. Some of your fellow students—including some from your own academic major—have already landed entry-level jobs in your field. If you are not talking to these successful peers to get their insights and advice for your own search, you are doing yourself a major disservice, for several reasons:

- These students know what their employers are looking for in new college graduates, so they can help you market yourself more effectively to their companies.

- These students have likely developed personal contacts with other companies as well—contacts they can share with you.

- In many cases, companies that have successfully hired students from one school or program in the past look for other students from that same school or program later on when more jobs are available. Why? Because, an employer will often reason, "If we found someone good at School X before, then we will go back to School X to find someone good again now." So by keeping in touch with your fellow students who have already landed jobs, you can position yourself to land an interview the next time those students' employers are hiring.

Your Family Members. I am always amazed by the number of college students and recent graduates who have never told their own families what type of job they are looking for. Then again, I am not—because I made the same mistake when I was in college and even after I graduated!

If you think about it, though, you are foolish not to make your family members aware of your career-related wants and needs. After all, they know people too, just as we all do, and those people probably work in a wide assortment of industries in a variety of geographic locations. So tell Mom and Dad—and Uncle Fred, cousin Tanya, your sister-in-law, and all the rest of your relatives—about the type of job you are pursuing. More than likely, they all want to help you anyway but do not know how. Give them a specific "how" and you just might be rewarded with some tangible leads.

Your Campus Career Counselors. Most every college and university in the country has a campus career center staffed by counselors who enjoy helping students plan for the future and find jobs. Their salaries are paid by you and your fellow students, through your tuition dollars and student fees. All of that is reason enough to tap a campus career counselor's expertise. But there's an even better reason as well: Campus career counselors are among the most well-connected people you will ever meet. They know all sorts of employers and all sorts of students and alumni, so they understand where the jobs are, who has them, and who is offering them. If you are in the back of a campus career counselor's mind when a great job comes along, that counselor will probably tell you about it—and not tell the many other students he or she has never met.

Your Professors. Like your campus career counselors, your professors know the key employers in your field. In many cases, they stay in touch with former students as well—students who are now succeeding in the world of work. Furthermore, many professors have consulting agreements and other business-related arrangements with various companies. It all adds up to information and contacts—both of which can help you in your job search.

When you are looking for a job, you cannot afford to overlook any resources, let alone your potentially best ones. So as you begin identifying the people who can be helpful to you in your search, do not look too far afield. Start your networking close to home.

Highlight This: The people right in front of you (literally and figuratively) could be the ones who steer you toward job-search success—if you remember to involve them.

It's Not What You Know *or* Who You Know—It's Both

Who you know will get your foot in the door. What you know will keep your foot out of your mouth.

Cajun proverb

An organization that hires a new college graduate for almost any type of position requiring a degree will spend at least $30,000 during that employee's first year if you include salary, benefits, and various recruiting costs like advertising the position, interviewing candidates, and conducting background checks on finalists. That number could easily double in relatively high-paying fields like engineering, computer science, and consulting. Employing people ain't cheap.

So if you really believe an organization will hire someone who is not qualified solely because his parents are good friends with the recruiting coordinator, you will almost certainly be wrong. The old cliché "it's not what you know, it's who you know" just does not hold up to scrutiny in most cases. Sure, there are exceptions to the rule, especially in large organizations where $30,000 can be absorbed much easier than it can be at a seven-person non-profit agency. But in most organizations, every single job matters. And as long as every single job matters, organizations will insist on hiring the *best* candidates.

Think about what is on the line for anyone trying to fill a job. Most people who hire as part of their organizational role are under considerable pressure—from their supervisors and other staff members alike—to get it right. Why? Because bad hires carry several costs that no organization wants to pay (and that most organizations cannot afford to):

Wasted Money. If you are a hiring manager and you bring on board a screw-up who ends up leaving—or being asked to leave—in a few months, you have just wasted thousands of the organization's precious dollars. For obvious starters, you convinced the organization to pay a few months' salary, not to mention benefits and perhaps other perks, to someone who turned out to be a bust. You might just as well have driven down the street in a limousine, throwing 20-dollar bills out the window for an hour; the result would have been the same. Moreover, you not only wasted all the money the organization invested in the initial recruiting and hiring process, but now you get to spend even more money—not to mention even more time and even more energy—going through the recruiting and hiring process all over again.

Staff Frustration. During the few months your screw-up hire was on board, perhaps he managed to alienate other members of the staff by missing deadlines, walking around like he owned the place, spouting ideas that were either ridiculous or already in place, and expounding on worthless knowledge and his weekend benders. Maybe he even managed to walk away from the copy machine when it jammed or to consistently pour himself the last cup of coffee without making more. How do you suppose the other staff members feel about this rocket scientist? Worse, how do you suppose they feel about you, the person who hired said rocket scientist in the first place?

Missed Opportunities. Perhaps your screw-up hire was supposed to be calling on prospects (via the phone or in person) to sell advertisements for the magazine your company publishes, but he was better at calling his girlfriend, playing Advanced Mine Sweeper on his computer, and singing along with the annoying songs coming through his online music feed. As a result, the September issue of your magazine will have 30 percent fewer ads than the August issue, accounting for thousands of dollars in lost revenue.

Suddenly, hiring someone solely because he or she has a "connection" is not looking too smart—or realistic. Now you know why, in most organizations, it is not what you know *or* who you know: it is *both*, at least ideally. The typical organization simply cannot afford to hire people who do not have the skills, experience, education, and traits to do the job at hand. That is not to say connections don't matter at all; they do, because employers know it is easier, faster, cheaper, and less risky to hire candidates they know or candidates who come highly recommended by trusted colleagues (see **Why Is Networking So Effective? The Reasons Have Little to Do with You**, p. 233.) But while "what you know" may, by itself, land you a job, "who you know" is not nearly enough on its own. "Who you know" needs its "what you know" sidekick if your job search is to end in success. And that goes for the hiring manager's best friend's daughter, too.

Highlight This: "Who you know" might get you an interview, but it will not—on its own—get you the job. You need to be competent for that to happen.

This Test Is Graded on a Curve

Concentrate your strengths against your competitor's relative weaknesses.

Paul Gauguin

You have probably spent most or even all of your academic life so far—10 years or more by now—being graded on a percentage basis:

- If you earn 90 to 100 percent of the points on a test or in an entire course, you get an A.

- If you earn 80 to 89 percent of the points, you get a B.

- If you earn 70 to 79 percent, you get a C.

- If you earn 60 to 69 percent, you get a D.

- If you do not get at least 60 percent of the points, you "earn" yourself an F.

This is actually a very fair and predictable type of grading system, for it puts you in full control of your own academic destiny. When I was in school, for example, I could be sure that if I actually did my calculus homework each day, studied for the midterm exam, and as a result scored a 93 percent on it, I would receive an A. If, on the other hand, I fell behind on my calculus homework, did not study for the midterm exam, and as a result scored a 26 out of 80 (33 percent) on it—not, ahem, that this ever really happened—I would get the F I deserved.

In short, the percentage system of grading is crystal clear and consistent. As long as you do what you are supposed to do and earn the necessary number of points, you will get the grade you want. It does not matter if no other students or a hundred other students do as well as you do: your grade is your grade based on what you and you alone have done or failed to do, as the case may be.

That said, I have some bad news for you: You will not be graded on a percentage basis in the world of work. Nope, this test is graded on a curve. In other words, the employer will not be comparing you to an arbitrarily selected number of *points*; he or she will be comparing you to other *candidates* who are vying for the same job (or internship or co-op) you are.

It all begins during the application review process, when the prospective employer is reviewing your résumé and cover letter along with the résumés and cover letters of God knows how many other applicants. As she sifts through the stack of paper—or, just as likely these days, she goes through the mounds of e-mails and their attachments—she will be comparing your stuff with everyone else's stuff. Your materials might have been stellar enough to earn you a B+ or even an A if you had submitted them in a career development course at your school. But if, in the employer's pile of résumés, there are one or two other candidates whose materials would have earned an A+, guess what: Your real grade just fell—to an F!

Huh?

Yes, your grade just plunged to an F. As in your résumé just got tossed into the circular File, also known as the recycle bin or the trash can—not because it was not good, but because *someone else's was better*.

So much for the 90-80-70-60 grading system.

The trend only continues from here. If you do make it into the "keep" pile of résumés—the people who will be invited in for interviews—you will again be going up against not a number or a percentage, but other candidates. You might walk out of your interview thinking, "I killed in there!" And maybe you did. But if just one of the other candidates "kills" better, or faster, or more convincingly, then you are the one who is dead. Your candidacy is now over. Your grade: F again. As in you have Failed to beat out the other candidates to win the job.

Suddenly, getting graded is a whole lot different than it used to be.

If you are ready for this new way of being evaluated, and you learn how to take advantage of it, you can still get your A—in the form of the job (or internship or co-op) you really want. Here's how:

Acknowledge to Prospective Employers Your Awareness of the Competition. Let employers know that you understand how they are "grading" you—and that you are both willing and able to compete for the best grade in the candidate pool. For example, suppose your cover letter included a few sentences that read something like this:

> I know you will be considering many candidates for this job, and that most of these candidates will make all sorts of claims about their skills and backgrounds. I want you to understand that, unlike these other applicants, I am prepared to *prove* the claims I will make in an interview with you.

With just a few well-chosen words, you have now practically dared the employer not to interview you for the job.

Ask Not "How Did I Do?" but "How Did I Do Compared to Others?" Whether you are developing your résumé and cover letter or getting ready for an interview, it is essential to get some feedback from an outside expert—a campus career counselor, perhaps, or one of your professors, or someone else who knows you a little bit but not so well as to assume anything about you. Suppose, for example, that you have just finished the umpteenth revision of your cover letter and you decide to show it to the recruiting coordinator at your school's career center. Do not just ask her, "How does it look?" Instead, nudge her to consider your letter in relation to others she has seen by asking her, "How does mine compare with those of other students you've worked with? Be brutally honest with me—will it compete with the best?"

Start Comparing Your A's to Those of Others. Next time you get an A on, for example, a major research paper, ask someone else you know in that class—someone who also got an A on the assignment—if you can read what he or she came up with. In what ways is this person's paper superior to yours? In what ways is yours superior to hers? If both of your papers were the finalists in an academic writing contest that would have only one winner, whose paper would win? Would you still get an A in that situation—that is, would you win?—or would your paper suddenly become an F?

Now you know how you have to start thinking during your job search. From here on out, the only grades awarded will be A's and F's. Which will you receive?

Highlight This: In college, you are competing only against yourself. In the job search, you are competing against dozens or even hundreds of other job seekers. You will receive one of two grades: an A (you land the position) or an F (you are turned down for the position).

Focus Is Critical to Job Search Success

If you chase two rabbits, both will escape.

Chinese proverb

One of the worst things you can say to a prospective employer, be it in your cover letter or in a job interview, is "I am open to most anything"—or any of its variations, such as "I am willing to give anything a try" or "I will do whatever you want or need me to do."

How can this be? Aren't employers looking for adaptable, resourceful workers who can handle any curveball that might be thrown their way? Yes, that is exactly what an employer wants from you—once you are hired and on the job. When you are still being *considered* for the job, however, what you are selling as your versatility comes across as just the opposite to most employers. Warning bells begin to sound as the employer immediately jumps to the conclusion—fairly or unfairly—that you are:

Unfocused. No one wants to hire a dabbler—a person who bounces from company to company or even career to career in an attempt to find the setting that (finally) fits. You may view yourself in the positive light of being flexible—the ideal employee. But rightly or wrongly, many hiring managers will perceive you in the negative light of being unclear and uncertain of what you want in an employer and a job.

Desperate. If you ever watched the old Bugs Bunny cartoons on Saturday mornings or after school, you will remember the classic episodes featuring a big, mean bulldog named Spike and his yappy terrier sidekick, Chester. Chester followed Spike around constantly, literally jumping in front of him and over the top of him saying things like, "What are we gonna do today, Spike?" and "Where are we gonna go today, Spike? Huh, Spike, huh?" Spike would stoically take Chester's antics for a few seconds before slapping the little dog away with the back of his paw. Chester's annoying reaction was to launch right back into his regular routine all over again.

Being on the receiving end of someone who strikes you as desperate is unappealing at best and slap-worthy (figuratively speaking!) at worst. Many employers will view your "I will do anything" routine the same way Spike always viewed Chester: as a nuisance. Once you have been identified by an employer—again, fairly or unfairly—as unfocused and desperate, you will automatically be classified as too risky to interview, much less hire. Your candidacy will be over.

Focus is critical to your job search success. Until you are clear about the type of position you are looking for and with whom, employers are likely to dismiss you. Moreover, you will end up wasting considerable time, energy, and even money sending out résumés or going on job interviews that ultimately lead nowhere.

You may not be able to narrow your job or company choices down to one or two. That is normal, not to mention perfectly OK. But you at least have to ensure that employers *perceive* you as being focused—by customizing your résumé and cover letter to each position you pursue, for instance, or by going into each interview prepared to say not "I will do anything" but rather "I want to work for *you*—and here is why."

Are you lacking clarity right now as you prepare to look for a job? Are you projecting the deal-breaking attitude of "I'm a risky hire"? Then it is time to get focused. Here are some ways to do just that:

Work with a Career Counselor at Your School or in Your Community. Career counselors have the tools, experience, and professional connections to help you start moving from fuzzy to focused.

Take a Career Planning or Job Search Course at Your School or in Your Community. Many colleges and universities, as well as some nonprofit agencies, offer credit or noncredit classes that can show you how to narrow your range of options.

Talk to People in Various Fields of Interest. *Informational interviewing* is a fancy term for talking to people to gather helpful information about a particular career, organization, or both. You may be only one or two coffee meetings away from the focus you need to be more successful in your job search.

Participate in an Internship, Do Some Temp Work, or Volunteer. You may be one of the many people in this world who learns best not by reading or listening, but by *doing*. Short-term opportunities like internships, temp jobs, and volunteerships exist, in part, to give you the opportunity to try out a job or even an organization without necessarily committing to it long term.

Phrases like "I'll do anything" need to disappear from your job-search lexicon. You need to replace them with phrases like "I'm interested in _____ and here's why." You will not be taken seriously by prospective employers until you commit to becoming committed.

Highlight This: Employers do not hire dabblers; it is far too risky. They are instead looking for candidates who know where they are going and why.

Perfect Your Approach

It Is Never Too Early to Start Your Job Search

Better three hours too soon than a minute too late.

William Shakespeare

If you are a college senior or you soon will be, when should you start looking for that first postgraduation job? The short answer is: today. But the slightly longer, more complete answer is: today, though it depends on what you mean by "look."

Suppose, for instance, that you graduate in May and that it is mid-November right now. You have more than five months until you walk across the stage to pump the hand of your school's president and pick up your degree. If you see an intriguing job in the newspaper or online and it is clear the company wants to fill the job immediately, you will more than likely be wasting your time and the employer's if you apply for it. You will not be available to work for months, after all, so it makes little sense, practically speaking, for you to pursue the position.

In other words, if you define "looking" for a job as pursuing positions that are open now and need to be filled immediately, it *can* be "too early" to start your job search. You really cannot do this type of looking five or six months out. If you are only a month or two from graduation, on the other hand, you can definitely apply for jobs that need to be filled immediately. Most employers need at least a month and sometimes two or three months to fill an open position. It takes time to advertise the job, receive applications, review those applications to select people to interview, interview the finalists, and make an offer to the candidate who has outshone all the others.

So if May is still five or six (or more) months away, do you just sit around listening to your iPod and drinking lattes until March or April? Not a chance. If you define "looking" for a job just a little more broadly and creatively, you will find that there is plenty you can do—starting today (no matter when today is)—to begin your job search.

Create a Solid Résumé and Cover Letter. If you plan to write your résumé and cover letter in 37 minutes the night before you apply for your first job in April, I have some bad news for you: Both your résumé and your letter are going to stink. Employers can spot rush jobs in milliseconds. You may have the talent to put together documents that *look* good and contain no typos. But if you want these materials to have solid content, then you will have to concede to the reality that quality takes time. You have plenty of time if it is mid-November and you do not graduate until May. Use it to develop a compelling résumé and cover letter, either on your own or, better yet, with the help of a counselor at your school's career center.

Talk to People Working in Your Chosen Field. If it is still November, for instance, you could use part of your upcoming holiday break to set up informational interviews with people— either in your college town or your hometown (depending on where you will be during break)—who work in the field you want to get into. You could even try to set up informational meetings with people who work at specific companies or organizations that interest you. No need to hit them up for a job outright. (That will just annoy them.) Instead, tell them you will be graduating in May and that you are simply seeking *information* and *advice*—nothing more. You will be surprised by how many people will agree to chat with you, especially immediately following the holidays, when things slow down a bit in many organizations.

Attend Professional Association Meetings. One of the simplest ways to stand out from the (large) crowd when you are a college student is to join a professional association in your field—particularly if there is a chapter in your area—and attend its meetings faithfully. So few college students bother with this strategy that you distinguish yourself when you do. Just as importantly, people working in your chosen field see you at the association meetings, quickly come to understand that you are serious about the industry, and get to know—and remember—you. Who is going to have an edge several months down the line when you apply for a position at Company X, whose hiring manager you have met several times at your professional group's meetings? Will it be the candidate the hiring manager has never heard of, or will it be you?

Monitor Job Listings in the Newspaper, Online, and Elsewhere. Just because you will not be applying for jobs immediately does not mean you shouldn't be watching for which positions are open and where. It does not take long to start spotting trends. You might figure out, for instance, that Company Y is in growth mode—and therefore may have an opportunity for you a few months from now—because it keeps posting employment ads that say "new position" in them. You will also be able to get a sense of the key skills, traits, and educational requirements most employers in your field are seeking and whether they are "preferred" or "required."

Read About Your Field and/or Organizations of Interest. Something as simple as reading the business section of your local newspaper each day can help you build a solid understanding of trends in your chosen field and developments within organizations that interest you. Add to your list industry-specific publications—which you can often read online—and you will soon start to develop a stronger sense of what is going on in your field and why. You will need that knowledge in your interviews a few months from now—assuming you do not want to look ignorant, of course.

On my Career Planning for College Students message board on MonsterTRAK (http://www.monstertrak.com), college seniors will often log in several months before they are set to graduate so they can ask their version of the question, "Is it too early to start looking for a job?" It is never too early—but it can easily be too late.

Highlight This: You cannot go wrong by starting your job search sooner versus later. But the specific strategies you use depend on how close you are to graduation day.

When in Doubt, Apply!

'Tis better to have fought and lost than never to have fought at all.

Arthur Hugh Clough

One fabulous way to waste your time and an employer's is to apply for a job that is well above your level of skills, education, experience, or all three.

Suppose you just completed your bachelor's degree in computer science, and your three-month internship this past semester convinced you the time was right to take a shot at a chief information officer (CIO) position. (Yes, some students do think this is reasonable.) The employer will likely react either by cursing your ignorance under his breath or, in a few cases, howling with delight and showing your résumé and cover letter to all of his colleagues—so that they can have a good laugh too, at your expense.

Probably not what you intended.

But what if the position you want to apply for is truly a close call—something you think you are qualified for one minute and unqualified for the next? To apply or not to apply—that is the question. There is an easy answer: apply. If you think about it for a minute, you will immediately understand why. If you apply for an iffy job and you are ultimately turned down—either at the screening stage or after an interview or two—then at least the *employer* made the decision. You gave yourself a chance to win the job; it may have been only a 10 percent chance or a 1 percent chance or a snowball's chance, but it was a chance nonetheless. Things did not work out, but you were in the running—albeit only fleetingly, perhaps.

If, on the other hand, you decide not to apply for the "maybe" job, then you give yourself a 0 percent chance of success; failure is a certainty. Instead of forcing the employer to consider you—if only for a few seconds—you leave the race. Indeed, you do not even get in the race to start with.

Now, granted, the definition of a "borderline" job will vary from person to person. You have to use your head when you are determining whether a particular position is a "maybe" job or not. In fact, you may simply want to try contacting someone from the organization advertising the position to see if the decision makers there are open to considering a candidate with your background, says Al Pollard, a recruiter with financial services company Countrywide.

"I say that for two reasons," stresses Pollard, who has also worked as a career counselor at the University of North Texas and as a recruiter for Enterprise Rent-a-Car. "The selfish reason is that it's tough enough to go through the people that qualify for the job. If you add a lot of unqualified people to the mix, that makes my job much harder." Moreover, Pollard points out, if you apply for a seemingly borderline job that wasn't quite as borderline as you wanted to believe, "then as a recruiter my perception is that you either didn't read the job posting or you don't value my time and don't follow directions well."

To apply or not to apply will rarely be an easy question to answer; there are simply too many variables involved, both on your side and the employer's. But if, after *full consideration*, you come to the conclusion that you have at least an outside shot of being taken seriously for the job, then by all means apply. At worst, you will get the old "thanks, but no thanks." Then again, you just might be surprised with an interview invitation.

Highlight This: If you cannot decide whether to pursue a particular job opening or not, adopt this seven-word motto: *better to apply than not to try*.

You Can Beat the Low GPA Blues

The least of the work of learning is done in the classroom.

Thomas Merton

You are reading an ad for the internship of your dreams and you appear to be qualified for the job. *Working toward a bachelor's degree in marketing or a related field*—check. *Junior or senior standing*—check. *Previous work experience required*—check. *Must be available to start June 1 and stay through August 15*—check.

GPA of 3.25 or above required—errrrnk! No go. Thank you for playing.

Many organizations that hire college students for internships and entry-level jobs use GPA as an initial screening tool. Indeed, in the *Job Outlook 2006* survey of employers conducted by the National Association of Colleges and Employers, a trade association for college career services professionals and employers of new college graduates, respondents gave GPA an average importance ranking of 3.5 (on a scale of one to five, with five being "extremely important"). In fact, more than 70 percent of the survey respondents said they screened college students for internships and jobs based on their GPA. GPA is not the *most* important indicator of your potential; but it is definitely *one* important indicator in the eyes of many employers.

So if your GPA is less than stellar, you may find yourself being eliminated from consideration for internships, co-ops, or jobs that would be a solid fit for you—unless you get a little creative. Now, "creative" does *not* mean lying about your GPA (as in the phrase, "The accountant got *creative* with the company's finances"). Aside from the obvious ethical problems with, ahem, neglecting to tell the whole truth, there is the very real risk that you will be busted sooner or later. If it is sooner, before you are hired or even interviewed for a position, not only will that employer blacklist you, but she will likely also tell her colleagues (in her own organization and elsewhere) to blacklist you. If you are caught later, on the other hand, after you have been hired for a position, the typical result is swift and embarrassing termination. Do not pass "Go," do not collect 200 dollars. You probably will not "go directly to jail," but you will certainly go back to your job search again, and fast.

So fiction writing is out where your GPA is concerned. What *can* you do? Plenty:

Focus on Your *Major* GPA. Perhaps your overall (cumulative) GPA is only 2.9 (on a 4.0 scale). But if you are like many students, your major-specific GPA—i.e., your GPA as calculated using the grades from courses in your major only—is significantly higher. You might have a 3.25 GPA or even better where your major classes are concerned. If that is the case, either use your major GPA exclusively when dealing with employers—indicating it specifically as such so that there is no confusion—or include it along with your cumulative GPA.

Calculate Your GPA for a Shorter, More Recent Time Period. Perhaps your freshman year was horrible in every way, and your grades from that time reflect it. But you came back strong sophomore year—not strong enough to boost your cumulative GPA above 3.0 (on a 4.0 scale), but close. Now that you are a junior, consider calculating your GPA for sophomore year and then trumpeting that figure with the employers you are approaching about internship or co-op possibilities. Sure, you might have had a 1.9 GPA freshman year, and your cumulative GPA might only be 2.7. But your sophomore-year GPA might well have been greater than 3.0 (it had to be if you bumped your cumulative GPA up to 2.7).

Get out your transcript and calculate the exact number. Then, if an employer wonders why your overall GPA is only 2.7, you have the ammunition to say: "That's true, but it is only because I got off to a rough start freshman year. Last year, my GPA was much better—3.1, to be exact. And I plan to continue in that direction."

Retake the Courses You Botched. At many institutions, you can retake courses if you have done poorly in them previously. Often, the only grade that counts in your GPA calculation is the higher of the two—presumably the one you will receive the second time around. This strategy can get expensive. You will not want to get into the habit of taking all your courses twice. But if a poor grade in one class is doing considerable damage to your cumulative or major GPA, retaking the course is an option you will definitely want to consider.

Play Up Degree of Difficulty. Is a cumulative GPA of 2.8 in an academically intense major like engineering the same as a cumulative GPA of 2.8 in a less challenging (in the eyes of some) major like sociology or physical education? Many employers would say "no"; they would cut you some slack for your 2.8 GPA in engineering, knowing how difficult those classes in physics and fluid mechanics are. So do not be afraid to point out your major's "degree of difficulty," be it in your cover letters or in interviews. Careful, though: Focus only on the difficulty of *your* major, not the perceived *ease* of other majors. Why? Because you have no idea what the employer you are dealing with majored in during her college years.

Find Ways to Market Yourself in Person. Employers typically use the minimum-GPA requirement in their screenings of prospective employees' written materials. Thus, if your cover letter or résumé lists a GPA of 2.9 (or lists no GPA at all) and the minimum required GPA is 3.25, you're toast. But often, if you can simply get in front of an employer, you can convince her you are a good candidate no matter what your GPA. So attend job fairs on and off campus. Ask your career center for help in setting up informational interviews with alumni and other working professionals. Put the word out to friends and family that you are looking for an internship or a job. Your low GPA is something you can overcome—if you can talk to an employer in person, face-to-face.

Grades really cannot—and do not—predict your future performance on the job. But for better or worse, they can most certainly predict whether you will get a chance to compete for the job in the first place. So make sure you get an A when it comes to portraying your grades in the best possible light.

Highlight This: Fairly or unfairly, your grades matter to many employers. If your GPA is too low, look for ways to either make it higher outright or put it in its proper context.

Customized, Carefully Crafted Documents Win Interviews—and Jobs

Words have to be crafted, not sprayed.
They need to be fitted together with infinite care.

Norman Cousins

When you are a career counselor, you see a lot of bad résumés and cover letters. It is the nature of the business. Just as mechanics tend to work on faulty engines and customer service reps hear more complaints than compliments, we career counselors spend most of our résumé and cover letter time spotting problems—some minor, others deal breakers—and doing our best to help clients fix them.

Frankly, it can get a little old sometimes and discouraging, too. So you tend to get more excited than the average bear when you see good résumés and cover letters. And you get even more pumped up when you think you have the rare chance to see a whole bunch of great résumés and cover letters at once. That is exactly what I was expecting back in 1997, when, as a graduate student at the University of Wisconsin-Whitewater, I was asked to be on a search committee to hire a new director of career services at the school. Whoever we hired for the job was going to be instrumental in teaching UW-Whitewater students how to put together solid résumés and cover letters. So I expected to see some exceptional résumés and cover letters from these director candidates. "After all," I figured, "who is going to write better résumés and cover letters than people who will be teaching others how to write great résumés and cover letters?"

Soon, there was a pile of candidate résumés and cover letters on my desk. I stopped everything to begin reading through
them. To me, it was going to be Christmas in February. Within
minutes, however, Christmas was a memory because D-day
(Disappointment Day) had begun.

A few of the documents were indeed outstanding—just what you
would expect to see from people competing to be director of career
services at a four-year, comprehensive university. But the rest of the
résumés and letters seemed to have been written by candidates who
were smoking an illegal substance at their keyboards. One person
in particular stands out in my mind, even to this day. Apparently,
the candidate had worked previously in a K-12 school—not in a
college setting. So his obviously photocopied (not to mention old)
cover letter talked about how he was the person who could best
help the "pupils" in our "school district." But we had *students*, not
"pupils"; and we had a *university*, not a "school district." Faster
than you can say "phoned in," this particular candidate was out of
the running in my mind. Others on the committee had the exact
same reaction to his lame application materials.

Another candidate—one who apparently watched a lot of
late-night infomercials on TV ("But wait! There's much, much
more!")—sent us a several-page diatribe, filled with exclama-
tion points, telling us what a mistake it would be to pass him by
for the job. His letter had the tone and feel of a carnival barker's
pitch: "Step right up, ladies and gentleman, and see the world's
greatest candidate for director of career services! Astounding!
Amazing! Nothing like it in the world! Don't miss it!"

Uh, we will take a pass, sir.

And so it went. Every fifth or sixth candidate—perhaps five
or six of them in all—sent us targeted, well-written cover letters
and résumés. The rest sent us various levels of garbage—almost
always the exact same photocopied garbage they had sent to some
other poor souls who were looking to fill a job. It was in many

ways a disappointing and demoralizing experience for me. But then again, I am secretly thankful for it in a way, because it taught me several important lessons about résumés and cover letters that you, too, need to understand before you begin your job or internship search.

When You Are an Employer, You Want People to Apply for *Your* Job in *Your* Organization. When you are faced with the task of looking through a stack of dozens or even hundreds of cover letters and résumés, you do not have the time to figure out how someone's generic documents address your specific needs. You demand that each candidate do this work for you. That is, you want each candidate to plainly and specifically show you how he or she is the best person for *your* job in *your* organization. Those who don't bother? You don't bother with them, either. You just toss their stuff into the recycle bin.

When You Are an Employer, You Can Spot Generic Documents from Two Counties Away. Even if you hire only one person a year, you quickly learn to see whose résumés and cover letters are written just for you and whose are generic copies that have emerged from the candidate's laser printer for the 107th time this week. Think about it. As a college student, you probably receive a hundred form letters from marketers for every individual letter you might receive from your school. How fast do those form letters end up in the garbage can?

So Few Candidates Customize Their Documents That Those Who Do Immediately and Automatically Stand Out. When I was on that search committee at UW-Whitewater, at least 80 percent of the application materials I saw were junk. How do you suppose that made the other 20 percent look—especially once I had read 20 or 30 sets of materials? When you see a quarter on the ground, glimmering in the sunlight, you stoop to pick it up. You do not even notice the rocks and dirt and ABC (Already Been Chewed) gum surrounding it.

It really does not take as much as you might think to grab an employer's attention with your cover letter and résumé. By simply customizing each letter and résumé you send out—even just a little bit—you will start to land more interviews. Yes, it is a pain. But would you rather invest your time, energy, and money in 150 resumes and letters that get thrown away, or five resumes and letters that blow employers away?

Highlight This: The power of the written word becomes even stronger when an employer can tell you have written your résumé and cover letter specifically for *her* and *her organization's* needs.

Use Numbers to Give Context to Your Accomplishments

Numbers are intellectual witnesses that belong only to mankind.

Honoré de Balzac

Perhaps numbers are your best friend. Maybe you are one of those people whose life would have no meaning were it not for the statistics pages in the sports section of the newspaper. On the other hand, maybe the last numbers you ever want to see—besides those on your paycheck or in your bank account—are the ones you cursed about every day in your Introduction to Linear Algebra course freshman year. Whatever your true feelings about numbers in general and mathematics in particular, know this: Numbers—even in very simple form (as in no vector calculus required)—will help you in your job search, particularly when you are sending out résumés and cover letters in an attempt to land interviews.

Why? Two reasons. For starters, numbers are *verifiable*. That is, if an employer sees a number of some sort on your cover letter or résumé, she can check it out, either before inviting you in for an interview or during her in-person conversations with you. It is difficult—not to mention risky and stupid—for job candidates to stretch the truth where numbers are concerned, and employers know that. One bad hire will cost any organization at least several thousand dollars (and often much more). So employers will always be looking for reassurance when they are considering various job candidates; numbers provide a bit of that reassurance.

But the real power behind numbers is the *context* they offer, both to the employer reading your résumé and cover letter and to you as the person trying to convince the employer to interview you. Watch what the addition of just one simple quantifier does to the following item, which you might find on a typical college student's résumé:

- Original: Trained new employees.

- Revised: Trained 15 new employees.

The original phrase is not bad, but the reader (an employer) has no context to go on. For all she knows, you trained only one new employee and you stunk either hated it so much you vowed never to do it again, or stunk at it so much that your supervisor vowed never to have you do it again. The revised phrase, on the other hand, gives the employer helpful context. What could she read into the number 15? Several things, potentially:

- You must have been pretty good at training new employees; otherwise, you would not have been asked to train so many of them.

- You must at least be able to tolerate, if not enjoy, training new employees.

- If the employer ever wanted to ask someone about your training skills, she would have at least 15 potential candidates she could track down.

Suppose you revised the phrase again so that it became:

- Trained 15 new employees in two weeks' time to prepare for restaurant's grand opening.

Now the reader has a time element to consider as part of the context. She might thus conclude, for example, that you perform well under pressure or that you manage your time effectively.

You do not need to be a rocket scientist (literally or figuratively) to use numbers to your job-search advantage. You just have to be aware enough, and willing enough, to find ways to quantify your various activities and accomplishments. Here's how:

Think in Terms of Money. For-profit and nonprofit organizations alike must worry about the bottom line. Whether the goal is to maximize shareholder profits or pay for food at a homeless shelter, organizations need money to survive and thrive. So whenever you can, paint your accomplishments with a financial brush. Examples:

- Raised $3,750 for a local child care center by organizing and hosting a two-day carnival on campus.

- Researched Internet service providers (ISPs) and recommended one that ultimately saved the company $1,400 the first year.

Think in Terms of Time. Save an organization time and you invariably save that organization money as well—not to mention intangibles like staff members' sanity. Remember, too, that time references on your résumé and cover letter give the reader critical context for understanding what you have done. Examples:

- Taught administrative assistant how to use "mail merge" function in Microsoft Word to automate printing of sales letters, reducing production time by 80 percent.

- Resolved computer users' troubleshooting questions (20 per day, on average).

Think in Terms of Quantities and Amounts. Did you do something once? Fine. But what if you did it dozens of times? What if you called *hundreds* of people instead of, say, three? Examples:

- Recruited 47 new members over two semesters, nearly doubling the organization's size.

- Contributed to the construction of four homes as a member of Habitat for Humanity.

Numbers can really add up where your job search is concerned. Go figure.

Highlight This: Your accomplishments will stand out even more to prospective employers if you use numbers to put them in their proper context.

On-Campus Recruiters Are Not the Only Ones with Job Openings

Not to know is bad; not to wish to know is worse.

Nigerian proverb

For the vast majority of America's employers, visiting college campuses to recruit students for internships and entry-level jobs is a waste of time, money, and energy. It is just not worth it.

It is not that you and your fellow students have nothing to offer, mind you. No, most employers stay away from college campuses because the economics of on-campus recruiting just do not make sense for them. Think about it. If you are someone who runs a small nonprofit, for example, and you have one unpaid summer internship to fill, why in the world would you spend an entire day (or two or three) interviewing students at a nearby campus career center when it would be far easier, faster, and cheaper to simply post your opening on that career center's Web site and interview prospects in your own office? Similarly, if you need to fill a job immediately because the person who had it yesterday quit today and will not be in tomorrow or any other day after that, you just do not have time to go the on-campus recruiting route; you have to find someone pronto.

Only a small minority of the employers that exist can make a solid business case for on-campus recruiting. These organizations tend to share several characteristics:

They Are Very Large. Sending one staff member to one school to spend one day interviewing students costs several hundred dollars at a minimum by the time you factor in the person's salary, travel time, lodging and food, transportation, and time away from his or her other work activities. Imagine, then, the huge organizational cost of recruiting students at more than one institution. You have to have some big-time money to pull it off—the kind typically found only in large organizations.

They Are from the For-Profit Sector. Most nonprofits, no matter what their size, simply cannot justify the expenses associated with on-campus recruiting. For-profit companies, on the other hand, can usually show that despite the initial high cost, on-campus recruiting pays for itself in the long run, in the form of better candidates who need less training and who stay in their jobs longer.

They Have Full-Time Recruiting Staff. In most small and many midsize organizations, hiring is done by supervisors, managers, and others who take on the task of filling positions as they come open. The typical large organization, conversely, has full-time recruiters whose sole job is to find new employees. Participating in activities like on-campus interviewing is written right into the typical recruiter's job description.

They Have Many Internship or Job Openings at Once. Some multinational companies hire several hundred interns and a few thousand entry-level employees every single year. (In 2006, for instance, Enterprise Rent-a-Car estimated it would be hiring 7,000 entry-level employees.) When recruiters from these companies visit college campuses, they are not just interviewing students for one or two positions but dozens and dozens of them. The more people your organization is hiring, the more cost-effective on-campus recruiting becomes.

They Can Forecast Their Hiring Needs Months Ahead of Time. If your school's career center offers on-campus recruiting, you will notice that many employers start showing up in the fall to recruit for the following spring and even the following summer. These organizations—which tend, again, to be large, financially strong, and in constant growth mode—can predict with reason-able certainty just how many college students they will need to bring on board six to nine months down the road. The typical small organization, meanwhile, often has a tough time pinpoint-ing what it will be dealing with six to nine *days* down the road. That is not better or worse than what you would find in a large organization; it is just different.

No matter where you go to school, you are surrounded by prospective employers. Draw a 200-mile radius around your col-lege or university and you will discover thousands of prospective employers, in fact. How many of these employers are coming to your school to recruit? A comparative handful, for all the reasons described here. But that does not mean the other employers do not exist and do not have opportunities you can pursue.

One of the myths most campus career centers struggle with—year in and year out—is the notion that they serve only business, accounting, finance, and computer science majors. Take a quick look at any campus career center's on-campus recruiting lineup and you will be convinced this myth is in fact a reality. Most on-campus recruiting schedules are dominated by organizations from the consulting, accounting, finance, technology, insurance, and car rental sectors. Why? It is not because they are the only industries the career center wants to serve, and it is certainly not because they are the only industries where jobs are available. There is no conspiracy against liberal arts majors here; these industries just happen to be the only ones that can financially justify on-campus recruiting activities. Others have to find employees in different ways.

So do not fall into the trap of believing that the only internships and jobs you can pursue are the ones organizations are recruit-ing for on campus. When you are looking at your campus career center's on-campus recruiting schedule, you are seeing only a few organizations of the thousands that exist, recruiting for only a few positions of the thousands that are offered. If one of those organizations and positions fits you, great. Sign up for an on-campus interview and see if you can win the job. But if none of those organizations and positions fits you, remind yourself that you are seeing only the tip of the iceberg. The much larger portion lies beneath the waters off campus.

Highlight This: Only a small fraction of organizations can make a financial case for recruiting college students on campus, and those organizations represent only a small fraction of the entry-level jobs available in the marketplace. Just because no one is coming to campus to recruit students in your major does not mean there are no jobs for students in that major!

Get Involved in a Professional Organization to Make Yourself Known

Professional associations are out there and they are loaded with resources that will jump-start your dream job.

Patrick Combs

I admire my colleague Martha Krohn from afar because she played her cards absolutely masterfully to land the job she wanted—so much so that when she looks back on her job search today, she says the practically unthinkable: "It was really easy."

Sound appealing?

The words "easy" and "job search" almost never go together. But because Martha had joined and gotten modestly involved in a professional organization in her field—almost two years before she completed her master's degree in counseling from St. Mary's University of Minnesota—her postgraduation job "search" was not really a search at all; it turned into a job *invite*.

I first met Martha in 2003, when she joined the Minnesota Career Development Association (MCDA) and signed up for an event-planning committee I was on. She was changing careers, she told me, from information technology (IT) to career counseling. She was just beginning her master's program, and she had joined MCDA so she could get to know people in the career counseling field in the Twin Cities—and, as importantly, so she could help some of those people *get to know her*. She did not jump into any kind of high-visibility, high-level role within MCDA. She just quietly but consistently showed up and got involved in small but essential ways—tracking a planning committee's spending here, helping coordinate a special event there. Before long, she was asked to run for the unpaid position of board secretary for MCDA. She did, and she was elected, thanks in no small part to her previous involvement with MCDA. People *knew* Martha and knew she was friendly, thorough, and dedicated. They had all seen those characteristics (and many more) with their own eyes, more than once.

Martha finished her master's degree just a few months ago, and like most new grads she immediately began her job search. It did not end up lasting very long, for she was soon being asked to apply for a position at the University of Minnesota's Humphrey Institute for Public Affairs. More accurately, she was being encouraged by the Humphrey Institute's director of career services, Lynne Schuman—for Lynne, you see, had just finished serving as treasurer of MCDA, a role through which she had not only met Martha but had also been witness to Martha's work, her spirit, and her dedication to the field of career development.

In short, the decision to recruit Martha was a no-brainer for Lynne: Martha was clearly a solid candidate for this particular job. She still had to prove it, though, by doing exceptionally well in several interviews and then presenting a résumé-writing workshop to a small group of Humphrey Institute students. She also had to beat out the other finalist for the job—"who had many more years of experience," Lynne says, "and was a dream candidate on paper." But thanks to Martha's involvement in the professional association that she and Lynne had in common, she was a known commodity where Lynne was concerned. "Being known got Martha in the door," Lynne stresses. "But it was her great performance in the interview process that made it possible for her to be selected over the better-qualified candidate."

Known commodities ultimately get jobs—and often, a known commodity's job search *is* "really easy," just as Martha characterizes hers. I like to remind Martha, though, that her "it was really easy" comment is not entirely accurate. "You *made* it easy," I counter. Like most of us Midwesterners, she is too modest to agree with me out loud. But I know she knows the real truth.

Would you like your job search to be "really easy"? Adopt Martha's approach and there is a good chance you will get your wish. It is not an easy strategy, and it is certainly not a quick one. Remember: Martha began executing her plan nearly two years before she would have to begin looking for a job. She knew—and accepted—the fact that her strategy would be a long-term one, not a quick-hitting, instant success.

She began—as can you—by finding the right organization to join in the first place. Professional associations exist for practically any field you can think of. And if you live in a fairly large city, you might well be able to find a nearby affiliate of the professional group you have your eye on—a local chapter of the American Marketing Association if you are a marketing major, for example, or a local chapter of the Association of Information Technology Professionals if you are a computer science major. You might even be fortunate enough to have a campus chapter of the group at your school.

Your first step, then, is to find and then sign up for a professional association that makes sense given your career goals. A counselor at your school's career center can help you identify possibilities. As a college student, you will almost always be able to join any group at a drastically reduced price compared to professional members who are already working in the field. It is not uncommon for a professional membership to cost, say, $150 a year while your student membership will cost you only 20 bucks. (After all, these groups want you to continue being a member after you have graduated.)

Once you have joined a particular organization, you are ready for phase two: getting involved in the group in some small but visible way. Volunteer to be on an event-planning committee.

Write an article for the association's quarterly newsletter. Offer to help with the redesign of the group's Web site. Figure out something—anything—you can do to contribute to the organization, and as a result become known within the organization.

Before long, you might well be like my colleague Martha—on your way to developing the credibility and visibility that lead to job *offers* instead of a job *search*.

Highlight This: Employers like to hire people they already know. One of the easiest ways for you to become known is to join and get involved in a professional association in your field.

Why Is Networking So Effective? The Reasons Have Little to Do with You

Sometimes students think networking is about who you know. But often it is about who knows you.

Bill Scott

You have almost certainly heard it before: Depending on which statistic you believe and where it came from, anywhere from 60 percent to 80 percent of all job seekers who end up finding positions land those positions through *networking* activities. Statistically speaking, networking is by far the most effective job-search strategy out there.

Ever wonder why?

The explanation, as it turns out, is only indirectly connected to you, the job seeker. What is the real reason networking is the best job-hunting activity *you* can pursue? The employer and, more specifically, what he or she is up against in trying to fill any open job within the organization.

Imagine yourself as a middle manager in a midsize publishing company. Say you oversee the editorial department for one of the magazines the company publishes. You are at your desk, trying once again to do too much with too little time and resources, when you hear a soft knock on the door.

"Come in," you say—only to immediately wish that you had pretended to be on the phone.

In walks one of the assistant editors of the magazine, with a piece of paper in her hand. Judging by the look of the document as well as the look on the assistant editor's face, you brace for the worst.

The assistant editor hands you the letter and the first line you read says it all: "Please accept my resignation from Company X."

You are neither surprised by nor angry with your now soon-to-be-departing assistant editor; you knew she would not stay around forever. So outwardly you congratulate her and tell her how much you and the staff will miss her. Inwardly, meanwhile, the stress is already beginning to build: You now have a key position to fill on your staff, and you do not have much time to waste considering your magazine is published monthly.

How will you proceed? Easy. You will just put a job listing in the local newspaper classifieds or on one of the major job search Web sites, then wait for the assistant editor's replacement to show up at your door—right? Wrong. Very, very wrong, in fact. If you are like most busy and somewhat skeptical employers, the newspaper classifieds and the job search Web sites will be about number five (or worse) on your list of preferred job-filling strategies. Why? For starters, one of the counterintuitive side effects of listing jobs in the paper or online is that people respond to the ads. When the comparatively rare diamond in the rough responds, it is wonderful. But too often, the people who respond are hopelessly underqualified for the job, hopelessly overqualified for it, or merely hopeless period. It is not at all uncommon for employers to receive hundreds or even thousands of replies to newspaper or online job postings. How fired up do you suppose they are about going through all of those applications? Many would rather walk over hot coals; it's faster and it doesn't hurt nearly as much.

Most employers—especially those from midsize and smaller organizations—are not made of money, either. Newspaper and online ads are often expensive; you are looking at spending a few hundred dollars, at minimum, in most cases. In return, you often get to waste hours or even days of your time combing through applications whose materials end up in the recycle bin (either the one on your floor or the one on your computer's desktop). So if you are the middle manager who needs to fill the assistant editor's position—fast—and you are understandably reluctant to list the job in the paper or online, what are your other alternatives? Chances are you will begin—and pray your task will end—with two closely related strategies: either hiring someone you yourself know personally, or hiring someone you do not know personally but who comes highly recommended by someone you do know personally. In other words, you will try to hire a "known quantity," either by tapping into your own network of contacts directly or asking your contacts for recommendations of other candidates you should interview.

Step back into your own shoes now. What if that poor middle manager who needs to hire an assistant editor—fast—has run into *you* several times at the state magazine publishing conference, and has made a point of reading your articles in the campus newspaper as a result? Alternatively, what if someone else he always runs into at the state magazine publishing conference in turn knows you thanks to an informational interview you conducted with her three weeks ago? When the middle manager asks his colleague for names of potential candidates for the position, your name will likely come up. And just like that, you are potentially in the running for the job.

If you are an employer, it is always preferable to fill a position via the back channel if you can (although there are obviously settings—particularly in the government and nonprofit sectors—where laws, policies, or both require you to advertise the position to the general public). It is easier, it is faster, and it is cheaper, for starters. But more importantly, it is far less risky. Even if you do go the route of listing a job in the paper or online, and then sifting through the respondents' materials, and then interviewing a few of the candidates, and then interviewing one or several of those candidates a second time, and then ultimately hiring one of those candidates, the person you bring on board is a relative stranger to you. What if he talked a good game in the interview but he ultimately winds up being an idiot that everyone on staff detests? (Yes, this happens, more often than you might think.) If, instead, you hire someone you already know pretty well—or, alternatively, someone who comes highly recommended by someone you know and trust—you reduce the odds that you are bringing on board the "staffer from hell."

So as you mull over the merits of networking during your job search, step outside your own mind for a moment and get into the employer's head. Are you beginning to see why the most appealing job-search methods for the typical college job seeker—namely, the newspaper and the Internet—are the options of last resort where employers are concerned? Yes, networking may sound unappealing to you; that is completely understandable. But you have to get beyond the old cliché "it's not what you know, it's who you know." For the more compelling and relevant question is this one: Who knows *you*?

Highlight This: Networking activities eventually help you become a known quantity to prospective employers—which is good considering that most employers hire known quantities over strangers.

Introverts Can Network Too

You have your way. I have my way. As for the right way, the correct way, and the only way, it does not exist.

Friedrich Nietzsche

If you are an introvert like me, the concept of *networking*—hell, even the word "networking"—is revolting. You want to get out there and network about as much as you want to go on *Fear Factor* and be lowered into a vat of earthworms while singing the karaoke version of a Barry Manilow tune. It is just too disgusting to think about, let alone do.

I understand, believe me.

But I also understand that, statistically speaking—and with common sense factored in as well—networking is by far the most effective job-search strategy out there. Employers much prefer to hire people they themselves know, or people who come highly recommended by people they themselves know (see **Why Is Networking So Effective? The Reasons Have Little to Do with You**, p. 233). So networking just has to be a significant part of your job-search repertoire, whatever your personality.

Fortunately, we introverts can adopt as our own a line from another hit song, this one popularized by the legendary crooner Frank Sinatra. Sing it with me now:

"I did it … mmyyyyyyyyyy waaayyyyyyyyyy!"

Yes, it is critical for you to get to know people—and, more importantly, to help them get to know you—during your job search. But no, you do not have to build relationships the same way extroverts do. If you are put off by the thought of donning a suit to attend a networking event where you shake people's hands with your right hand and give them your business card with your left, then don't go. If you feel like making cold calls to employers actually worsens your chances of getting a job because you perform so badly on the phone, then don't make them. Sure, you will continue reading about these strategies in the career articles and books you have been looking at, and people around you will undoubtedly continue nagging you about them. But if they do not fit you, why use them? Instead, play to your natural strengths and try networking strategies like these:

Use Your E-mail. I am convinced that e-mail was invented by an introvert. I cannot prove it, but it makes perfect sense to me, for several reasons:

- E-mail allows you to think as long as you want to before you "speak" (with your keyboard, obviously). It is hard to be caught off guard or stumped when you are talking with someone via e-mail.

- E-mail allows you to contact people—even total strangers—without feeling like you are bothering them or making them angry. To some degree, it even allows you to get to know people before you ever actually meet them in person. (Fact: I have worked as a consultant for online career site Monster since 1999; I have yet to meet anyone I work with there in person. We do everything via e-mail and the occasional phone call.)

- E-mail has led to the invention and growth of Internet *listservs* and *discussion groups* where you can "talk" to a bunch of people at once without being in a room with a bunch of people at once! I am on a career counseling listserv, for example, where I can easily post questions to my career counseling colleagues. (Where do you suppose many of the quotes and examples in this very book came from?)

If it takes less energy for you to contact and talk to people with your fingers instead of your mouth, then use your fingers instead of your mouth—at least for your *initial* interaction(s). You can always arrange to actually meet with someone in person later.

Set Up Informational Interviews. If you are like most introverts, you much prefer one-on-one conversations over group interactions. You would rather focus on one person at a time—in depth—and in turn have one person focus on you. "Working a room" just takes way too much energy. Moreover, you would rather not feel like you are putting pressure on someone and hitting him up for a job. That is the beauty behind *informational interviews*—informal chats with people working in a field(s) of interest to you. You can e-mail someone and ask if he or she would be willing to, for example, meet you for coffee so that you can ask for some information and advice. Or, you can simply "talk" to the person via e-mail itself (see **You Do Not Need to Talk to People in Person**, p. 40).

Join a Professional Association in Your Field and Get Involved in Some Behind-the-Scenes Way. My friend, colleague, and business partner Pamela Braun—who is even more introverted than I am—used this strategy masterfully. I got to know her when she and I both joined the Minnesota Career Development Association. But she did not come running up to meet me and shake my hand, nor did I run up to her. Instead, she volunteered to be the editor of MCDA's quarterly newsletter, a role that gave her name recognition among the members of the organization without her having to shake a single hand or utter a single "nice to meet you." I saw that Pam was the newsletter editor and e-mailed her—naturally—to see if she could use contributing writers. We ended up getting to know each other a bit via our e-mails before we eventually met in person for the first time at MCDA's annual spring conference. Now we are business partners—and, ironically, one of our specialties is helping our fellow introverts in the job search.

Like all job seekers, you need to network to give yourself the best possible chance of actually landing a position. But you do not need to network the same way an extrovert would. We introverts can network too—if we do it oooouuuuurrrrrr wwwaaaaaaayyyyy!

Highlight This: Networking is essential for all job seekers, but introverts do not have to—and undoubtedly will not—network the same way extroverts do.

Perfect Your Presentation

Presentation Is Everything—Make Sure You Look Good, on Paper and in Person

> *First appearance deceives many.*
>
> Ovid

Whenever you meet someone new during your job search—whether it is in an interview or at a meeting of your professional association, and whether you are introducing yourself face-to-face or via a written document—what you *say* in the first few seconds (or sentences) is practically irrelevant. How you *look*, in person and on paper, will solidify the new person's view of you, for better or worse.

Take your résumé, for example. In a 2005 survey of 72 employers conducted by the Career Masters Institute—a national association of career development professionals—participants stressed that the best way for a job seeker to make a good first impression with his or her résumé is to make sure it is "easy to read *at first glance*" [emphasis added]. In-person judgments are made just as quickly. In 2000, University of Toledo psychology professor Frank Bernieri (who is now chair of the psychology department at Oregon State University) led a study in which individuals were videotaped during job interviews. The first 10 seconds of each tape were then played for a group of UT psychology students—whose reactions ended up closely matching the reactions of the interviewers who had gone through eight pages of questions with each of the job candidates. The study, Bernieri noted at the time, was the first "to offer proof that you never get a second chance to make a first impression."

So beginning today, you need to take a critical look at how you are presenting yourself to the world of work. You will almost certainly need some help on this task from a trusted but brutally honest friend or an experienced counselor at your school's career center—someone who will have no hesitation about telling you your résumé is an eyesore or your interviewing wardrobe is liable to make you eligible for a witness protection program.

Start with the easy stuff: your written documents, namely your résumé and cover letter. Look for common presentation problems like these:

Wall-to-Wall Text. Suppose you have two books open in front of you. One is *Moby-Dick* and the other is *The Cat in the Hat.* Which one is a more inviting read? This is not a trick question: You would choose *The Cat in the Hat* in a heartbeat, in part because it features fewer words and those words are presented in a more graphically pleasing way than is the case in *Moby-Dick.*

Now, suppose you are an employer and you have two résumés in front of you. The first is a one-pager written by a job seeker who has clearly gone out of her way to make her document readable at a glance. The document features comfortable margins all around and some white space between various sections. The second is a two-pager that is practically all text. It features quarter-inch margins and no obvious white space between sections. Which document is the more inviting read? Again, it is not a trick question: The résumé that is easy on the eyes is the résumé you will look at as the employer. You will set the other one aside—either for the moment or forever.

Inconsistent Formatting. When you are driving on the interstate and you see a green sign with white letters, you know it will give you information about a road or a city that lies ahead. Over time you have learned that all green highway signs with white letters serve this purpose. Suppose that rule suddenly changed without your knowledge. Now you are driving along in a strange place looking for your exit and you pass a blue sign with white letters—the type that normally signifies a rest stop, only this time it offers the exit information you need. You ignore the sign; you are looking for a green one, after all. Five miles later, you finally realize you missed your exit, thanks in great part to the inconsistency in signage.

The very same thing will happen to the prospective employer who tries to read your inconsistently formatted résumé. He will look at the first section—"Experience," for instance—and see that you have bolded and centered the title of the section. He will thus expect the other main sections of the document to be signified by a bolded and centered word or phrase. But the next section of your résumé—"Education," for instance—features a title that is underlined and flush left. Guess what: You have just confused the employer—and a confused employer is a frustrated employer who tosses your résumé aside and looks at the next one instead.

Lack of Visual Eye Catchers and "Resting" Points. Employers love résumés they can quickly glance through. They hate résumés they have to actually read; they just do not have the time. So if you are including a list of skills or accomplishments on your résumé, use bullets instead of a paragraph format. Which of the following is easier to read quickly, at a glance?

Served as vice president of Student Finance Association. Participated in student management of university endowment fund. Initiated area's first chapter of Students in Free Enterprise and led group of students who planned its regional conference.

OR

- Served as vice president of Student Finance Association.

- Participated in student management of university endowment fund.

- Initiated area's first chapter of Students in Free Enterprise and led group of students who planned its regional conference.

Bullets, used sparingly, enhance a document's readability. The same is true of bolded items, subheadings, and tabs and indents—again, all used sparingly.

Once you have revamped your printed documents, take a long, hard look at yourself: your clothing, your hairstyle, your jewelry and piercings, even your breath and your overall smell. (You may be stinking up your interviews because, well, you are stinking up your interviews!) Your clothes have to be clean, pressed, and appropriate given the industry and organization you are pursuing. Use perfume or cologne sparingly or, better yet, not at all (since some people have allergies to certain chemicals). Your hair must look the way *employers* will expect or even demand it to look, and your piercings and/or tattoos should be subtle, hidden, or nonexistent. In short, will an employer conclude that you look the part of the job you are applying for and the field you are trying to get into? Remember: He might not particularly care about your presentation where he himself is concerned; heck, he may be sitting in front of you wearing blue jeans and a sweatshirt! But he is asking himself a key question where you are concerned: "Could I unleash this person on a customer or client without embarrassing myself or, much worse, the organization?"

Is it fair for the book called you to be judged by its cover? Of course not. But it is reality. None of us has the time or the inclination to operate any other way. So when you are searching for a job or an internship, you have to look good, on paper and in person. Moreover, you have to look *consistently* good. If your résumé sends the message "highly professional" but your wardrobe screams "just rolled out of bed," employers and networking contacts will assume the worst about you, not the best. You are only as good as the lowest common denominator of your overall job-search appearance.

Highlight This: The way you and your job-search documents look is at least as important as what you and your job-search documents say.

Examples Beat Mere Words in Your Job Search

Extraordinary claims require extraordinary evidence.

Carl Sagan

The interviewer who asks the question "What are your strengths?" has heard responses like the ones that follow dozens, hundreds, or perhaps even thousands of times (depending on the length of her career and the number of people she has interviewed):

- "I'm a good team player."

- "I have strong communication skills."

- "I have a solid work ethic."

- "I'm flexible and adaptable."

- "I'm great with people."

- "I'm self-motivated; I take initiative."

- "I'm good at problem solving."

All of these responses and others like them might strike you as solid answers. When you consider them on their own, they *are* solid answers. But when you are a hiring manager and you have heard them repeatedly from candidate after candidate after candidate on résumé after résumé after résumé or in interview after interview after interview (isn't repetition aggravating?), you start to roll your eyes after a while. You become especially skeptical after you have hired one or two of these folks and they have gone on to demonstrate the exact *opposite* attributes once on the payroll. Indeed, every employer out there has been burned at least once by a candidate who dazzled during the interview but fizzled on the job.

That is why your words alone will not move the typical employer. You have to have something to back up your claims—examples and evidence that will convince the employer of the validity of what you are saying.

It all begins with your written documents. Take your cover letter, for example. If you were an employer reading through dozens of cover letters, which of the following cover-letter paragraphs would be most believable?

Candidate 1

I have strong communication skills, a solid work ethic, and outstanding flexibility and adaptability. I'm also self-motivated, good at problem solving, and able to work well with other members of a team.

OR

Candidate 2

I gained national recognition for my communication skills last year when I received an Honorable Mention award for editorial writing from the College Media Advisors association. I also demonstrated my self-motivation and teamwork skills by leading a small group of students who completely redesigned the campus newspaper over the course of three months.

The second paragraph obviously does not make as many *claims* as the first paragraph does. But it far outshines the first paragraph in its use of specific examples. It would be quite difficult, in fact, for an employer to ignore the second candidate, whereas it would be quite easy for the employer to toss the first candidate's letter into the recycle bin as another case of "Boy, I wish I had a nickel for every applicant who says this stuff."

Your résumé, of course, is the other key job-search document where examples beat mere words. Compare the following résumé items from Candidate 1 and Candidate 2:

Candidate 1

● Called alumni for university fund-raiser.

OR

Candidate 2

● Raised more than $10,000 in donations by conversing with alumni for university's annual phone-a-thon; polished ability to "soft sell" potential contributors.

Again, Candidate 2 has done the much more convincing job. For all the employer knows, Candidate 1 may have called only one or a mere handful of alums—raising no money whatsoever before giving up in frustration. Candidate 2, conversely, has put forth a specific dollar figure that the employer, if she wants to, can easily verify. Moreover, Candidate 2 has offered evidence of what she calls her ability to soft sell, versus merely *saying* something like "I am good at the soft sell."

You can adopt this same examples-beat-words strategy in your interviews, too. Put yourself in the employer's shoes one more time. You have just interviewed two candidates over a period of 90 minutes. Here is how each responded when you asked, "Why should I hire you and not one of the other candidates for the job?"

Candidate 1

Well, I want the job the most and I have strong communication skills, a solid work ethic, and good problem-solving skills.

OR

Candidate 2

For starters, I want the job the most. To prove it to you, I have put together this small binder of materials that I would like to leave with you. In it you will find some examples of my previous work along with a few ideas I have for contributing to your company's bottom line. I also invite you to contact not only the references I have given you, but also any other people who know me and have worked with me. They will all tell you that I am a self-motivated team member. Finally, I am prepared to show you my communication skills right now; if you would like, I will write up a mock news release for you or put together text for a 30-second ad. Just give me an hour or so and you will be able to see what I can do.

Candidate 2 may not be as brief as Candidate 1, but who cares? Candidate 2 is not only more confident-sounding than Candidate 1, but she has also put Candidate 1 to shame—again—by using *evidence* to argue why she should be the person hired for the position.

Just as jurors in a court of law are swayed by evidence (and unmoved without it), so too are employers convinced by evidence. Give them the examples they are looking for and you will be the candidate who makes it through the résumé screening, shines in the interview(s), and ultimately lands the job.

Highlight This: It is one thing to *tell* an employer you *can do* something; it is another thing completely to *show* the employer you have *already done* something.

Portfolios: Proof of Your Claims

The path of sound credence is through the thick forest of skepticism.

George Jean Nathan

Rick Nelles is a Minneapolis-based professional recruiter who has interviewed and hired thousands of people in his 25-year career. When you talk to him, it quickly becomes clear that he is a fountain of information on success in the job search—but from the comparatively unique perspective of someone who actually hires people for a living. He could write a book on how to land a job. Come to think of it, he has—two of them in fact (*The Career Performance Portfolio System: Build Your Ladder to Career Success*, Beaver's Pond Press, 2005; and *Proof of Performance: How to Build a Career Portfolio to Land a Great New Job*, Impact Publications, 2000). Both books draw heavily from Nelles's extensive experience in the hiring trenches.

Interestingly, though, while Nelles could talk for hours about the nuances of the job hunt, he can distill his simple yet profound advice to job seekers into a single sentence: "Employers won't believe what you say—on your résumé or in your interviews—unless and until you prove it."

Employers, Nelles says, have simply been burned too many times by candidates who, ahem, were not completely truthful during the application and interviewing process. They are also frustrated, Nelles says, because they cannot even check candidates' references anymore; the typical organization in today's litigious society will confirm only a previous employee's past employment ("Yes, she worked here") and nothing more. "That's why résumé fraud is at an all-time high," says Nelles. "Slick Willies and Fast Annies have figured out that they can lie on their résumés. So hiring managers these days are skeptical—big-time."

How can you address that skepticism as a college student seeking an internship, a co-op position, or an entry-level job? Just go back to Nelles's 19-word mantra: "Employers won't believe what you say—on your résumé or in your interviews—unless and until you prove it." You can offer that proof, and pick up some nice side benefits as well, by creating a *career portfolio* and using it in every single one of your interviews.

Perhaps you have heard of portfolios before. Most art and graphic design students are required to showcase their work in portfolios, as are some students in majors like advertising and public relations. In a nutshell, a career portfolio is a professional-looking three-ring binder filled with artifacts from your past that serve as evidence of your key skills and traits—the proof of performance that so many of today's employers demand to see before they will hire you. Think of it as the most valuable scrapbook you will ever put together—a scrapbook that can include:

- Letters of recommendation or commendation that you have received (from professors, supervisors, and others).

- Awards you have won.

- Articles you have written or for which you have been interviewed.

- Photographs connected to key achievements (e.g., a picture of you participating in the service-learning fair at the student union).

- Brochures you have developed, printouts of Web sites you have created, or posters you have designed.

- Brief stories you have written up to describe key achievements or to highlight essential skills like leadership, teamwork, organization, and presenting.

Unlike the fairly rigid requirements of your résumé and cover letter, your career portfolio's look, feel, and content are entirely up to you. Best of all, you can make your portfolio as long—or as brief—as you would like. "One of the big myths about portfolios is that they have to be long. But I stress quality over quantity," says Carmen Croonquist, director of career services at the University of Wisconsin-River Falls, and a portfolio expert who has presented on the subject from Minnesota to California to Iceland. "Even five or six quality items," Croonquist says, "can make a difference."

Especially when you have exclusivity on your side. Indeed, so few job seekers know about—let alone bother creating and using—career portfolios that you will immediately stand out to employers simply by having one. Your portfolio will also serve as a handy prop that will help you present yourself effectively during interviews, especially since it will boost your confidence beforehand. "That's really one of the beauties of the portfolio: It's a job-hunting tool, yes, but it's also a tool that can help you identify or recognize your own skills and accomplishments," says Nelles. "Most of us are so close to our own skills and accomplishments that we don't even see them in ourselves."

You cannot go into interviews not knowing your own skills and accomplishments. And you certainly cannot go into interviews without evidence of those skills and accomplishments. A career portfolio will serve both essential functions for you—so that you are the rare candidate who does not merely tell employers what you can do, but *shows* it.

Highlight This: If you are looking for an attractive, creative way to offer employers evidence of your key skills and accomplishments, a career portfolio is the tool for you.

Practice Makes Perfect Where Interviewing Is Concerned

He that would perfect his work must first sharpen his tools.

Confucius

You just finished a 90-minute interview for your first postcollege job. You are leaving the company's spacious building right now and walking out to your car, feeling a mix of relief and excitement, concern and curiosity.

If you are like most people, dozens of questions are already racing through your mind, most of them centering on a common theme: "How did I do?" You are also giving yourself a mental pat on the back for your solid responses, and, perhaps more troublingly, you are kicking yourself in the imaginary behind for the things you wish you had said but did not. The entire experience unfolds all over again like an instant replay, and it only continues during the drive home and on through the rest of your day. By the time a few hours pass, you have developed a fairly detailed opinion of what you did well in your interview and what you could have done better.

Wonderful! But there is a problem—two of them, in fact. For starters, this particular interview is now behind you, not ahead of you. Your postgame analysis, though admirable and understandable, will do nothing to help you win the position you just interviewed for. More importantly, though, your analysis is inherently biased because, well, you are analyzing yourself—a scenario that inevitably leads to an overdose of back patting, butt kicking, or both. What if you had done all of this thinking *before* the interview, with the help of an outside observer who could assess your interviewing strengths and weaknesses more objectively? You could have, by simply visiting your school's career center and asking one of the counselors there to conduct a *mock interview* (or two or three) with you.

A mock interview, for the record, is not an interview where a career counselor sits across from you and mocks your responses to questions. (I once worked with a student who had avoided mock interviewing thanks to her mistaken belief that she would be putting herself in the path of reactions like, "That's the dumbest answer I have ever heard in all my years of career counseling!") A mock interview is, quite simply, a practice interview—a full dress rehearsal (literally and figuratively) before the real thing—conducted by a career counselor from your school or, in some cases, a real employer who volunteers for the task through a special program set up by your school's career center.

Here is how the typical mock interview works. First, you set up a day and time to have your mock interview. The process might be as informal as arranging a half-hour meeting with a counselor at your school's career center. Or it might be as formal as signing up for the career center's annual Mock Interview Day, when dozens of employers—many of them alums—return to campus to help current students boost their interviewing skills. In either case, you can specify the type of job for which you would like to practice interviewing. You can even submit a real job listing from a real organization if you want to, so that whoever ends up serving as the interviewer for your mock interview can come up with realistic questions ahead of time.

Once your mock interview is scheduled, you prepare for it just as you would a real job interview. You study the organization you are "applying" to as well as the position you are trying to land. You do your best to predict what questions you will be asked, and you try to prepare the best responses possible. You might even rehearse a few of those responses with your roommate or one of your parents. Then you go to the mock interview itself. In many cases, the counselor or employer serving as the interviewer will go immediately into his or her role, just as soon as you walk in the door. The two of you will then go through a set of questions and answers, just as you would in an actual interview, before parting ways (or pretending to, at least) with a handshake once the session is done.

But your mock interview is not over yet; in some ways it has just begun, for you will use the remaining time with your interviewer to get his or her feedback on your performance. You will get an *objective*, third-party assessment of what you did well and what you need to work on before you go on a real interview. In some cases—depending on what you arranged beforehand—you may even watch a videotape of your interview performance, which your interviewer can use to not only give you feedback about your responses, but also to assess your appearance and spot any distracting habits you need to break, such as fidgeting or looking away from the interviewer too often.

Just as a professional golfer is best able to diagnose swing problems on the driving range with her coach, you will be able to iron out the wrinkles in your interview performance by working with a career counselor or another expert before you actually sit down in the hot seat across from an employer. Practice really does make perfect—in golf and in job interviewing.

Highlight This: The more you practice interviewing, the better you become at it. Just don't do your practicing during real interviews!

Out-Research Your Competitors, Win the Job

What is research but a blind date with knowledge?

William Henry

The more you know about the organization you are interviewing with—and the more you can demonstrate that knowledge to your interviewers—the better the chance you will be the person selected for the position. Why? Because the employer will correctly conclude that the person who knows the most about the organization—and can prove it—is likely the one who *wants* the position the most, who can bring the most to it, and who is willing to do the most to earn it.

"Researching the company before the interview is perhaps the single most important step for a new graduate to take to stand out from others," noted Marilyn Mackes, executive director of the National Association of Colleges and Employers, in commenting on NACE's *Job Outlook 2005* survey of 254 employers nationwide. "Despite the fact that information about organizations is easy to come by—through the Internet, in campus information sessions, and through company literature provided to the campus career center, for example—employers tell us that too many job candidates neglect to do their homework."

Knowledge is power in interviews—and lack of knowledge is an almost insurmountable weakness. Thus, you can beat out your competitors by simply out-researching them. Here's how:

Study the Organization's Web site. Little more than a decade ago, there was no such thing as a company Web site. Now, there is practically no organization without one. An employer will expect you to have looked carefully at the organization's Web site for basic information on its products and services, customers, goals, and mission. But be sure to search as well for newsier information—for example, the corporate newsletter or magazine, the organization's press releases, and links to organizational mentions in various media.

Ask the Organization to Send You Its Annual Report. Every publicly owned company and every nonprofit organization in the United States is required to publish an annual report of its earnings and activities. Request a copy before your interview, or see if it is available on the organization's Web site. Ask too for company brochures, employee or consumer publications the organization publishes, and any other printed resources that might give you some insights. (Again, these documents might well be freely available on the company's Web site; look for them.)

Page Through Various Directories in Your Career Center or Campus Library. Most campus career centers and libraries have copies of such directories as the *Thomas Register of American Manufacturers* and *Standard and Poor's Register of Corporations, Directors, and Executives* (both of which are also available online). These directories and others like them feature different information (so ask a career counselor or librarian for specific guidance), but all of them will help you gather additional data on the organization you are researching.

Use Online Company Research Sites. The World Wide Web is filled with sites that can help you conduct research on organizations of interest. Vault.com (http://www.vault.com), for example, has "insider" information on more than 3,000 companies and 70 industries, while Hoover's Online (http://www.hoovers.com) bills itself as offering "in-depth coverage of 40,000 of the world's top business enterprises." Wetfeet (http://www.wetfeet.com) and Monster (http://www.monster.com), among other sites, also feature information on companies and organizations.

Track Down Articles in Newspapers, Magazines, Newsletters, and Other Periodicals. Companies large and small make the news day after day. You can find that news on your own or with the help of a campus reference librarian, who can teach you how to use online databases such as Lexis/Nexis, ProQuest, and ABI/INFORM. Each of these databases indexes thousands of periodicals, so finding information on the organization you are pursuing is as easy as typing in a few well-chosen keywords or phrases.

See a Campus Career Counselor. Career counselors at colleges and universities work with dozens, if not hundreds, of employers each year. As such, they know a great deal about various companies and organizations, especially local ones. They can also help you identify and contact people working for and with these organizations.

Consult Your Professors. In their continuing quest to find students and new graduates for internships and entry-level jobs, employers will often contact professors directly, in hopes of getting an inside track on the best and brightest students. Thus, professors in your academic department are likely to have knowledge on at least some companies and organizations you are interested in. Be sure to tap into that expertise.

Take a Trip to the Public Library. This strategy will be particularly handy if you are looking for company information that is more than four or five years old. Many public libraries maintain "clip files" containing newspaper and magazine articles on various organizations. Because of its age, the hard-copy information you will find in these files may not be available online or in any other form.

Researching companies and organizations takes considerable time and effort to be sure—time and effort you could certainly devote to other activities. But the investment you make in gathering information will pay off when you are one of the few applicants—perhaps the only one—who really understands the organization, what it needs, and how you can help meet those needs. That is the type of knowledgeable person employers hire.

Highlight This: If you know more than other candidates do about a prospective employer's activities, goals, and problems, you will be in the best position to discuss how you can help the employer complete those activities, achieve those goals, and solve those problems.

Interviewing Is a Two-Way Street

If you don't ask, you don't get.

Mahatma Gandhi

A job interview can seem like a day (or two or three) on the witness stand in a criminal trial. You might feel like the poor sap who was on every single episode of the old *Perry Mason* series. You know the one: the person being questioned so fiercely by Mason that he or she melodramatically confessed to the crime right then and there ("All right! Yes, it was me! And I'd do it again, too!"), thus demonstrating the innocence of Mason's client and proving once again that (cue intimidating music) Perry Mason always gets his man (or woman).

Or maybe you have seen war movies where the prisoner is taken into a windowless, cinder-block room, shoved into a chair, dragged under a hot lightbulb, and "encouraged" to tell his captors what he knows: "Confess!" (slap) "Confess!" (slap, slap) "Confess!"

No wonder most college students—and most job seekers in general, for that matter—hate interviews.

But if interviewing was supposed to be a one-way conversation, it would just be called "viewing." The *inter* part of the term, after all, means "between." In other words, treat an interview like the two-way street it was constructed to be. Yes, your interviewers get to question you, but you get to question the interviewers too. An interview is meant to be a conversation between you, a prospective employee, and the organization, a prospective employer.

That is not as outlandish a concept as you might think. Put your-self in the employer's position for a moment. Do you really want to offer the job to a candidate who has asked no critical questions dur-ing her interviews with you? Probably not. Consider the risks:

Is She Interested? How can you be sure this candidate even wants the job? You may end up offering the position to someone who will ultimately turn it down, thus wasting valuable time that you could have used to offer the job to another candidate.

Will She Stick Around? The U.S. Department of Labor esti-mates that the cost of replacing one employee is one-third to one-half the value of that employee's annual salary and benefits. Ouch. So if you offer the job to this candidate and she takes it, how do you know she will still be around a month from now? If she does not start trying to assess her compatibility with the organization until *after* she is on board, and she then discovers she indeed does not fit in, she will probably quit—and you will be right back where you started, only several thousand dollars in the hole and looking like a dolt to your staff and your supervisors alike.

Will She Succeed? What if this candidate is not completely confident about her ability to do the job, even though she looks great both on paper and in person? She may end up taking the job and failing in it, hurting both herself and you in the process.

Of course, you are not the employer in a job-interview situa-tion. You are the candidate. You are a person who not only has goals, needs, and concerns, but who also deserves the chance to achieve those goals, meet those needs, and address those con-cerns. You are going to be giving 40 or more hours of your week to this organization, after all. In return you will receive a salary, of course, and perhaps an assortment of benefits, too. But what about the other forms of "pay" you might want or even need? Will you be able to advance at this company? You will not know unless you ask. Does this company live up to the work-life balance claims it makes on its Web site? You will not know unless you ask. Where will this company be five years from now? You will not know unless you ask.

Now, just as you do not want to be grilled like an accused criminal in your interview, the employer does not want to be interrogated either. Polite, respectful questioning is the order of the day. You are not a police detective or the state attorney general, nor do you want to be. But you are someone who is risking just as much as the employer is—more in some ways. So you deserve to know what you will be getting in an employer, just as she deserves to know what she will be getting in you.

Highlight This: Employers are not the only ones who should be asking questions in your job interviews. You have an obligation to yourself to ask questions of your own too.

The Power of a Simple Thank-You Note

Silent gratitude isn't much use to anyone.
Gladys Browyn Stern

Shortly after my wife landed her first professional job in special education back in 1992, she discovered the surprising power of a simple thank-you note.

By this time, she was a few months into her new role and she was getting to know her supervisor well enough to informally shoot the breeze with her when things were slow. So one day when the two of them were chatting, up came the subject of how my wife's position had been filled several months before and how she had been competing against several other good candidates. Why did she ultimately get the offer, especially when it could have easily gone to one of the others? One key factor, as it turned out, was that my wife had been the only person to send a thank-you note to her future boss and co-workers after the interview was over. None of the other candidates had bothered. And so that one seemingly small, almost insignificant act of gratitude stuck out when it came time to choose who would get the job offer and who would not. Moreover, my wife's boss remembered the gesture with a smile months after the fact.

The thank-you note is perhaps the most underappreciated and underutilized job-search and interview tool at your disposal, believe it or not. The thank-you note you send could literally spell the difference between getting the job or getting a rejection letter.

Why bother with this seemingly old-fashioned gesture? For starters, by simply sending your interviewers a thank-you note of any kind, you will put yourself among a surprisingly small group of candidates. Indeed, in a 2005 survey by MonsterTRAK (http://www.monstertrak.com)—the Web site for college students and recent graduates from leading career Web site Monster (http://www.monster.com)—72 percent of participating employers said they expect students and grads to send a thank-you note after an interview, but only 62 percent of the participating college seniors said they went ahead and sent thank-you notes after their interviews.

Keeping up with the Joneses, though, is not the only reason for sending a thank-you note—not even close. Your thank-you note can be just as strategic and compelling as your cover letter and résumé were when you initially applied for the job. Indeed, you can use your thank-you note to:

Reemphasize One or Two Key Points You Made During Your Interview. "Please keep in mind that, as I mentioned during my interview," you might write, "I have considerably more experience than the typical recent college graduate when it comes to the inner dealings of politics at the state level. As I discussed briefly near the end of our conversation, my internship with Senator Johnson gave me the key ____ skills you are looking for in the person you hire for this job."

Use your thank-you note to briefly jog your interviewer's memory about something you stressed during the interview. A sentence or two will help your interviewer remember what you said—especially if she interviewed several candidates for the job and you are all running together in her brain at this point.

Mention Something You Forgot to Point Out During Your Interview. I can safely say that after each and every job interview I have ever had, I have almost instantaneously thought of something else I wish I had said during the interview. (Usually it happens before I have even reached my car after walking out of the building.) If this happens to you, your thank-you note gives you a chance to redeem yourself. For example:

I was kicking myself after our discussion yesterday because I forgot to mention something that is important for you to know: I have some fund-raising experience, thanks to the volunteer work I did for my school's alumni foundation. Each of the last two spring semesters, I made phone calls to alumni on behalf of the school. During that time I was responsible for bringing in a total of $____ in pledges.

Confirm Your Continuing Interest in the Job. Professional salespeople often talk of the *close*—the time during a sales transaction when the salesperson actually attempts to finalize a sale. Most people who interview for a job either close poorly or, much more often, do not close at all. That is, they do not come right out and say—at the end of the interview—that they want the job. So a sentence like this one in your thank-you note could turn out to be quite compelling:

Thank you again for discussing the ____ position with me yesterday. I just want you to know that I continue to be interested in the position, and that I will be ready to start as soon as you need me.

Will a thank-you note, by itself, win you a job offer? Probably not. But it will tell the prospective employer that you are courteous (and that you will likely be courteous with his or her company's customers as well). More importantly, your thank-you note might well serve as the final piece that successfully completes the puzzle that is your job search.

Highlight This: A thank-you note after an interview is not only common courtesy, it is also a way for you to make one last memorable impression on the employer.

All Sorts of Factors Impact Your Job Search Success (or Lack Thereof)

Crises and deadlocks, when they occur, have at least this advantage:
They force us to think.

Jawaharlal Nehru

If you ever need a mechanic to fix your car, do not—I repeat, do not—contact me. Not if you want your car to be fixed, that is. I may be one of the worst would-be mechanics on the planet. I scored in the 15th percentile on the CAPS (Career Ability Placement Survey) test, meaning that in a roomful of 100 people, 85 of them would be better than me when it comes to understanding and solving mechanical problems. I was probably fortunate to score as "high" as I did considering the fact that I was unable to correctly answer the sample question before the real test began.

There is a reason I am a writer and career counselor; mechanics just isn't my thing.

But I do know enough good mechanics—including my own father and both of my brothers—to understand that when it comes to solving mechanical problems, the key to success is a comprehensive and systematic approach. You have to first determine each and every thing that could be wrong; you then have to painstakingly assess each of these potential bugs to determine which of them is the culprit (or which of them are the culprits, as the case may be).

At least once a month, someone on my Career Planning for College Students message board on MonsterTRAK (http://www. monstertrak.com) asks a version of the following question: "I'm doing everything I'm supposed to do to land a job [or an internship or co-op], but I'm not having any luck. What am I doing wrong?"

Sound familiar? If so, just like a mechanic you need to take a comprehensive and systematic approach to diagnosing and solving your problem. That involves identifying what could be wrong and then painstakingly determining which of these potential problems is the real roadblock (or which are the roadblocks, as the case may be).

At least eight factors could be at work:

The Position(s) You Are Applying For. Are you aiming for jobs that are appropriate for your level of education and experience? For example, are you continually trying for positions that require three to five years of experience when you are a brand-new graduate with only a summer internship's worth of experience? Or are you trying to get a job as an entry-level accountant even though you do not have an accounting degree?

Your Résumé and Cover Letter. Both your résumé and your cover letter need to be flawless and compelling if you want them to compete with the résumés and cover letters of other applicants. Are your documents superior? How do you know? Have you had them critically evaluated by, say, a campus career counselor, or a few of your professors, or, best of all, someone who actually works in the company or industry you want to get into? It is one thing to impress your roommate or your mother with your résumé and cover letter; it is another to impress a prospective employer, especially when he or she is reading not only your documents but the documents of dozens or even hundreds of others as well.

Your Follow-Up Skills. Are you contacting prospective employers—when appropriate—to make sure they have received your application materials and that they have everything they need from you to consider you for the position? Conversely, when the job ads specifically tell you *not* to call the employer to follow up, are you doing so anyway—and thus aggravating him or her to the point of not considering you? Meanwhile, after any interviews you have had, have you sent thank-you notes to the people who took the time to meet with you? If not, they may have concluded you do not care about the position, or that you do not have good people skills—or both.

Geography. Are you looking for the type of job that is almost always found in a larger, urban area even though you live in a city of only 6,000 people? Sure, there may be a few of these positions in your small town, but the odds are definitely against you. Similarly, perhaps you are applying for jobs hundreds or thousands of miles away but are offering prospective employers no evidence that you are willing and able to quickly move to that company's area—on your own dime—to take the position should it be offered to you.

Your Grades. For better or worse, fairly or unfairly, your grades matter to many employers (not all of them, but many of them). If the job ad in front of you reads "3.25 cumulative GPA required" and you send in your application materials knowing you have only a 2.95 GPA, you are wasting your time, energy, and money—not to mention the employer's. You w ill not be considered for the job, no matter how much you might wish and hope for otherwise.

Your Attitude. It is quite common—and it is human nature—for you to start feeling a little desperate when your job search is not going well. The problem is, that desperation almost always comes through on the employer's side of the table. The cover letter you send, for example, might fall into the trap of *asking* the employer *for* something (i.e., the job) instead of *offering* the employer something (i.e., your skills and experiences). Note the difference between the following objectives on a college student's résumé:

> **Objective:** An accounting internship that gives me the chance to gain experience, use my skills, and advance.

Objective: An entry-level accounting job that requires proven skills in accounts payable, accounts receivable, and budgeting.

The first objective is all about the student: me, me, me. The second speaks clearly to what the student can bring to the employer. It is a huge difference, especially in the employer's mind.

Lack of Evidence. Every employer out there has been burned at least once by an applicant who claimed something on a résumé or in an interview and then failed to deliver on that promise once hired. Thus, most employers are skeptical about the claims you make, and they will be expecting you to provide evidence to back up those claims. Suppose two students send in their résumés for a co-op position at a small public relations firm. Each of their résumés features a "key strengths" section near the top. Which of the following statements in that section is more compelling and offers more evidence?

Dedicated to the field of public relations.

Nominated by previous supervisor for "Intern of the Year" award given by local chapter of Public Relations Society of America.

The second statement offers the indisputable evidence the employer is looking for.

Your Interviewing Skills. Perhaps you are not having trouble getting interviews for positions, which suggests your résumé and cover letter are indeed solid. But after your interviews, you either never hear from the employer again or you get depressing rejection letters. Your interviewing skills might need some significant work. Have you done some practice interviewing (*mock interviewing*) with, for instance, a counselor at your school's career center? Has anyone given you critical feedback on your interview performance? Again, it is one thing to get feedback from your mother or your roommate, but it is another thing entirely to get feedback from someone who will deliver no-holds-barred commentary.

You may have some tinkering to do where your job search is concerned. You might even need to replace your current job-search strategies entirely. Do it on your own if you can. But if you are like me—if you need a skilled mechanic to help you do the job right (and to prevent yourself from doing further damage)—then get some help from a campus career counselor, a professor, a previous employer, your parents, or anyone who knows what he or she is doing. Sometimes you need an outside expert to get yourself back on the road.

Highlight This: When your job search is not going well, many factors could be to blame. Ask a campus career counselor or another expert to help you diagnose the problems.

Epilogue

There Is No Need to Go It Alone: 10 Reasons to Visit Your Campus Career Center

Refusing to ask for help when you need it is refusing someone the chance to be helpful.

Ric Ocasek

The idealistic part of me would love to believe that *Career Wisdom for College Students* has answered every possible question you could ever have regarding your future career. But then there is the realistic part of me, as well as the skeptical part of me, that gets incredibly irritated when any career success book claims it can solve every single problem of every single reader, as though we are all mindless robots who merely need to have the right buttons pushed to determine which career path to take, and why and how.

Well, we are not robots. This is not the era of *The Jetsons* (although sometimes it feels like we are getting closer). We are humans with brains and emotions, and each of us faces different circumstances that profoundly affect our career exploration and decision-making activities. No book—no anything—could possibly cover career development in both the breadth and depth necessary to fully address *your* particular career issues, *my* particular career issues, or *anyone's* particular career issues. Books can make a solid contribution—and I certainly hope I have accomplished at least that much in *Career Wisdom for College Students*—but they are not enough.

Fortunately, when you are a college student, help—free help, no less—is readily available to you at your school's *career center* (which may go by one of several names, such as *career development center* or *career services office* or *placement office*). Never heard of it? You are not alone. Many college students have no idea of the campus career center's existence; many others have only a vague memory of the career center from an on-campus tour or summer orientation, and have long forgotten the details of what the center has to offer. And that is a shame—because as many recent (and not-so-recent) college graduates will tell you, the career center is by far the most useful resource on your campus when it comes to helping you envision and achieve your future career goals. In fact, it is not a stretch to say that, on some campuses at least, the career center is the most important and valued student service period. Perhaps that should not be surprising given the results of a 2004 *Chronicle of Higher Education* survey, which found that most college students today go to college primarily for career-related reasons.

So if—make that when—you have career-related questions and concerns that go beyond the scope of this book or any other resource, head for your school's career center. If you need a reason, I will give you 10:

It Is Staffed by People Who Are Professionally Trained to Help College Students with Career Issues. Most campus career counselors (who usually call themselves *career services professionals*) hold master's degrees in counseling or a closely related field, and many have additional educational background that focuses on college student development issues. Moreover, some campus career counselors have worked in the corporate or nonprofit sector as well, so they can give you a sense of what to expect in the real world of work, especially when it comes to key job-search activities like preparing résumés and cover letters and getting ready for interviews.

Its Employees Work Closely with the Employers Who Will Someday Hire You. Career services professionals are very well informed on employment trends, in great part because they are talking with employers—in person or on the phone—practically every day. They also keep up on career-related trends through their professional reading and involvement in professional organizations. Careers are their career, and they can pass some of their considerable knowledge on to you.

It Is the Best Place on Campus to Crystallize Your Future. One of the many misconceptions career centers must fight is the notion that they are the place to go only when you are about to start your job search. Most career centers also focus extensively on career planning issues—helping you learn more about yourself (e.g., your interests, skills, values, personality), what is out there in the world of work, and even how you might put certain majors to career use (in answer to the common question, "What can I do with a major in _____?"). In other words, the career center can help you not only with "How will I get there?" questions but also with "Where am I going and why?" questions.

It Is Stocked with Career Resources, Whether in Print or Online. Among other things, most career centers offer job and internship listings, information on careers you might pursue with various majors, information on specific companies and organizations, and even (in some cases) information on the jobs and salaries of past graduates from your school. Many career centers also house libraries filled with books and periodicals that address various career concerns. All of these resources will help you learn more about the employment possibilities that exist in the world of work and which ones might fit you best.

The More Known You Are to the Career Services Staff, the Better the Chance a Staffer Will Refer You to an Employer. Let us be clear here: It is not a campus career counselor's job to "get" you a job. Nor is it ethical for him or her to play favorites among you and your fellow students. But picture yourself as a campus career counselor for a moment. If you saw a student in your office once a week learning about the field of, say, marketing, wouldn't you be more likely to at least mention that student to a company you know of that is looking for a marketing intern or full-time employee? Needless to say, it does not hurt for you to be in the back of a campus career counselor's mind when he or she is working with employers looking to fill positions.

It Offers Seminars, Workshops, and Courses That Will Lessen Your Anxiety and Confusion. Even the smallest campus career centers offer seminars and workshops, along with for-credit or noncredit courses, where you can learn about the entire range of career issues that will impact you during and after college. One of the nice side benefits of attending these programs is that you meet other students who share your worries. Whether you are a freshman or a senior, you are not alone in your anxiety and confusion about careers. By participating in your career center's programs, you will meet peers who are in your shoes. You can then help each other by tossing around career ideas, critiquing each other's marketing materials (i.e., résumés and cover letters), and perhaps even making each other aware of companies and organizations that might be hiring college students or new grads for internships, co-ops, or entry-level jobs.

It Can Connect You with People Who Can Offer Information, Advice, Opportunities, or All Three. Some campus career centers have elaborate databases of alumni who have offered to serve as career resources to current students like you. Some career centers bring alums and others to campus for career fairs, mock (practice) interviewing events, career exploration events, and more. Practically all career centers work with a core group of employers who have internships, co-ops, or jobs to fill. You can connect with all of these people quite easily by simply visiting the career center.

It Uses Technology to Meet Your Needs. Most campus career centers have now automated their job and internship listings so that they are available online. But that is not all: the cutting-edge career center of the mid-2000s also offers webinars (Web-based instructional seminars), podcasts (audio or video broadcasts covering career issues), listservs (electronic "discussion" forums), electronic newsletters, and live-chat question-and-answer services.

It Offers Career Assessments of All Kinds. Practically every career center in America offers pencil-and-paper or, increasingly, online versions of interest inventories, abilities and skills tests, and personality assessments. As I cautioned earlier in the book (see **This Is a Test; This Is *Only* a Test**, p. 11), no career assessment is going to "tell" you what you "should" be when you grow up. But many of them do a fantastic job of helping you understand yourself better and giving you career ideas to explore in depth.

You Are Paying for It! If you can think of no other reason to use your school's career center, consider the thousands of dollars flying out of your pocketbook each semester and into the coffers of your college or university. Your tuition and fee dollars help to pay for campus career counselors' salaries as well as all of the equipment and resources in the career center itself. In other words, you help fund the career center and everything it has and does—so you might as well take full advantage.

Most campus career counselors (myself included) go into the narrow field of career services and the broader field of career development because they genuinely want to help people like you who are wrestling with career issues of some sort. Often, campus career counselors (me included) struggled with career issues themselves, especially in the years during and immediately after college. To say they empathize with your situation is often a considerable understatement. But you will not benefit from their passion and expertise if they do not know who you are. And they will not know who you are unless and until you stop by to introduce yourself.

So put down this book and head for your campus career center. You have already invested some of your (or someone else's) money in this valuable resource. If you invest your time and energy in it as well, you will earn an outstanding return: the career wisdom that leads to future success and happiness.

Additional Help

One of the beauties of the Information Age is that you have access to hundreds of potential resources anytime you want to learn more about a particular topic. One of the curses of the Information Age is that you have access to hundreds of potential resources anytime you want to learn more about a particular topic! Where do you begin? How do you proceed when you are liable to catch the information overload virus at any time?

That is what this intentionally brief section of *Career Wisdom for College Students* is for. Instead of focusing on quantity and listing dozens upon dozens of resources for you to investigate, we instead focus on quality and offer you a few of the best resources—online and in print—for college students who are wrestling with career exploration and decision-making issues.

If what you need does not appear here (or does not seem to), visit your school's career center—because what you need probably *is* out there ... somewhere.

Web Sites
MonsterTRAK (http://www.monstertrak.com)

MonsterTRAK is the Web site for college students and recent graduates produced by leading global career site Monster (http://www.monster.com). MonsterTRAK features hundreds of original career articles (written by Yours Truly and others) geared specifically and exclusively to college students and recent grads. While you are there, check out the Career Planning for College Students message board as well, where you can post career-related questions and participate in discussions with your fellow college travelers. Oh, and by the way, you can search for jobs and internships on the site too!

Occupational Outlook Handbook (http://www.bls.gov/oco)

Every two years the U.S. Department of Labor's Bureau of Labor Statistics publishes an extensive guide to occupations. Each of the more than 250 occupational entries in the *OOH* features detailed information on what the job entails, the skills and education it requires, its future outlook, and more. Anytime you are in the beginning stages of investigating a particular job title or field or industry, the *Occupational Outlook Handbook* is one of the best places to start.

Quarterlife Crisis (http://www.quarterlifecrisis.com)

This site is the companion of Alexandra Robbins's, and Abby Wilner's outstanding 2001 book, *Quarterlife Crisis: The Unique Challenges of Life in Your Twenties*. The site features articles, several high-traffic message boards, and other resources geared to twentysomethings who are feeling a little lost where their careers (and perhaps the rest of their lives) are concerned.

Books

Ferguson Publications (http://www.fergpubco.com)

The *Career Opportunities* Series

The *Career Opportunities* series features more than 20 books, each of which describes 60 to 100 job titles in the field it covers. Among the wide-ranging topics: health care, travel, publishing, and fashion.

Morem, Susan. *101 Tips for Graduates*. New York: Checkmark Books, 2005.

————. *How to Gain the Professional Edge.* 2d ed. New York: Checkmark Books, 2005.

How can you prepare yourself for a fantastic career once you have graduated from college? Sue Morem answers that question—and then some—in these two books. Her book *101 Tips* covers the essentials of communication, leadership, and social interaction in the workplace. *Professional Edge* focuses on the behaviors and attitudes that will open the doors to your advancement and ongoing success.

Ferguson Publishing. *Encyclopedia of Careers and Vocational Guidance.* 13th ed. New York: Facts on File, 2005.

Look for this comprehensive five-volume resource at your school's career center or your campus or public library. It will be worth the effort, for it features information on 741 careers in 93 industries! It is the most comprehensive career reference tool in print. Yet it is easy on the eyes, too.

Other Helpful Career Books Geared to College Students and Recent Grads

Carter, Carol. *Majoring in the Rest of Your Life: Career Secrets for College Students.* 4th ed. Denver: LifeBound, 2005.

Combs, Patrick. *Major in Success: Make College Easier, Fire Up Your Dreams, & Get a Very Cool Job.* 4th ed. Berkeley, Calif.: Ten Speed Press, 2003.

Marriner, M., N. Gebhard, and J. Gordon. *Roadtrip Nation: A Guide to Discovering Your Path in Life.* New York: Ballantine Books, 2003.

Krueger, Brian D. *College Grad Job Hunter: Insider Techniques and Tactics for Finding a Top-Paying Entry-Level Job.* 5th ed. Cincinnati: Adams Media, 2003.

About the Author

Peter Vogt, M.S. has a passion for helping young adults find careers with purpose and personal meaning. His philosophy of encouraging college students and recent grads to identify and explore career possibilities while challenging their self-limiting beliefs, assumptions, and perceptions is born out of his experience as a career services professional at both the University of Wisconsin-Whitewater and Edgewood College, as well as his partnerships in College to Career, Inc. (a Twin Cities company that helps the parents of college students become solid career coaches to their sons and daughters, http://www.collegetocareer. net) and Campus Career Counselor, LLP (a Twin Cities career consulting and publishing company, http://www.campuscareer counselor.com).

As the MonsterTRAK Career Coach for MonsterTRAK (http:// www.monstertrak.com)—the college student/recent graduate Web site of leading global career site Monster (http://www.monster. com)—Peter writes weekly career advice articles for students and recent grads. He also answers dozens of questions each month on MonsterTRAK's Career Planning for College Students message board, which enables him to offer career guidance to students and grads from across the United States and around the world.

As publisher of *Campus Career Counselor* (http://www.campus careercounselor.com)—a monthly national newsletter for college/university career services professionals—Peter identifies and reports on the innovative ways campuses are helping college students and recent grads with career-related concerns. Additionally,

Peter has written articles for *National Business Employment Weekly*, *Managing Your Career*, and CollegeJournal.com and CareerJournal. com (both produced by the *Wall Street Journal*). He has also been interviewed as a career expert by the *New York Times, U.S. News & World Report, Time* magazine, *Ladies' Home Journal*, and the best-selling book *Monster Careers*.

Peter holds a master's degree in counseling from the University of Wisconsin-Whitewater and a bachelor's degree in mass communications from Moorhead State University. He lives in suburban Minneapolis.

Index